Confessions of Grace:
My Survival Guide

Melanie Thurston

CONFESSIONS OF GRACE:
My Survival Guide

Copyright © 2024 **Melanie Thurston**

ISBN (Paperback): 978-1-964494-25-8
ISBN (Ebook): 978-1-964494-26-5

Printed in the United States of America.

PROMINENT
BOOKS
EDGE

5830 E 2nd St, Ste 7000 #9983
Casper, WY 82609
USA

Acknowledgements

WELL, I GUESS if I'm writing an acknowledgements section I'm going to go through and publish this…whew. Honestly, that makes me break out in a cold sweat just thinking about it!

First and foremost, above all and everyone else, I have to thank God for giving me the strength and courage to actually write this book. This isn't what I would have thought I would do with my spare time… or without His prompting. In all honesty, I wouldn't be alive if it weren't for His mercy and grace. I wouldn't be the person I am without Him. His grace has amazed me for a long time and I'm fairly certain the longer I'm on this earth the more it will continue to do so. Also, where would I be without salvation through His son Jesus? I shudder to think!

To my Hoob, my husband Franky, who when I mentioned that God was prompting me to write a book never batted an eyelash. His faith in God is astounding. Where I struggle many days with faith, his seems unwavering. He pushed me and prayed for me. He took over lots of cooking duties so I could write and still work. When I mentioned I thought this book was going to be the death of me, he prayed harder for Satan to stay off my back. We have had some very hard, very discouraging moments in our 26 ½ years together, but we're still standing, and I am thankful for him!

To my children…oh the lessons you have taught me!! I feel most days I just suck at this role in my life. I've been the working parent and I've missed so many precious moments with all of you, it makes my heart hurt. Kaitlyn—for so many years I prayed for your healing and for God to make you whole. It's taken me years to realize you are as whole in your own way as I am; even though you are different, and your needs are different, you are not less. Erica—my sweet, thoughtful, sensitive girl—you amaze me in your own way. Your artistic soul does not always jive with my logical one, but you are kinder, sweeter, and more compassionate by nature than I'll ever be! I pray that you never lose that spirit! Nat(alie)—my little Newt—many times I think you're me made over but raised kinder. My little ride or die, gospel music loving, goofy and sarcastic kid—you make me laugh. Your prayers touch me. Your enthusiasm for Jesus at your young age awes me. I love each and every one of you fiercely!!

To my best friend, Wendy—what can I say?? I mean seriously—32 years of friendship with me should have you renting space in the nearest asylum, but here you are still seeking out times to spend with me. HA!! Many moments of "what had happened was" "we have regrets" and "we can't ever tell ANYONE this one" over the years. So many moments of love and laughter. Texting for hours, on the phone for hours. Venting, encouraging, laughing till we cry and nearly lose bladder control, but in the end, somehow, we still keep pointing each other to Jesus. May we have many more NQC conventions and trips to Gatlinburg together and lots more time to binge listen to Triumphant podcasts. God bless our poor beleaguered husbands!!

To my other best friend, Kristen—so many moments. I'm smiling thinking about them! We have, in so many ways, dragged each other through some of our hardest moments of life. But those moments where we laughed like hyenas? Yeah, those. I'll never forget you literally lying on my kitchen floor laughing. Everyone needs a friend like that!! And oh, the times at the altar praying and clinging to each other. May God richly bless you, my friend. You'll never know how much I love you.

To my many other friends who encouraged me to write this…why?? Seriously though, thank you from the bottom of my heart. I'm not sure why you thought it would be worth reading and I surely hope you too do not have regrets after reading it!! Apparently, my Facebook posts are amusing enough you thought I could drag it on for a hundred or so pages and it would work out!

To all my gospel music writers and singers—thank you for writing, singing, and performing inspiring, amazing music. Your music helps feed my soul and brings comfort to not just me but hundreds and thousands of others. There are so many to acknowledge personally—I'm going to pick one group and one soloist. Eric Bennett with Triumphant Quartet—what a strange way to build a friendship! I was and am still touched by how truly kind you were to my shy little girl at her first NQC (for those not familiar, that's the National Quartet Convention; it's an amazing gathering of gospel artists!) that I started following your group more. What I've seen is what many will echo—you are consistent, you love Jesus, and you preach and teach Jesus at every. Single. Opportunity. Thank you for being willing to read this mess and offer up suggestions and encouragement with my writing. Thank you for writing your book and following God's leading. Never in a million years would I have dreamed of this path, but here we are!! I am blessed by your friendship. To the other members of Triumphant—Clayton, Scotty, and David—you guys are some of the kindest, sweetest people I have ever met!! Your singing and songwriting talents are God given and amazing, but you always give the credit to Jesus. Scotty, thank you for letting me use "How Saved I Am" in this book—thank you for writing it, for listening to God's leading. Thank you for being so nice to not only me but every person who comes up and talks to you at your table!!

Also, Joseph Habedank—thank you so much for allowing me to use one of your songs, "This Grace", in my book. Thank you for your transparency and your testimony; thank you for being willing to allow God to use what could have been your downfall and turning it into yours and Lindsay's amazing story! Your testimony spoke to me so deeply, as it has so many others; it is so clear you are as in awe of God's grace as so many others are, and it translates into your music! And you, too, have shown such kindness to my little Gospel loving girl—I've seen you show that same kindness to many others as well!! Thanks for starting me on such a deep love of Southern gospel; thank you for your boldness and allowing God to use your story to highlight His grace.

To my amazing coworkers and church friends—how can I thank you enough?? Both groups of you, en masse, have seen me at literally my worst moments and for some reason you still have shown me such love and kindness. In your own ways, you have echoed mercy and grace to me, and I am overwhelmed with thankfulness to all of you. I pray I have been even a small amount of blessing to you all as you have to me!!

To my sweet friend, Linda Burgess, for taking on the project of proof-reading this book—you not only took on the endeavor with enthusiasm, but with your sincere love and kindness that I know of you. Thank you for your encouragement; I don't feel worthy of your kind words. A million times thank you. To Zachary—my "borrowed" son—thank you SO MUCH for doing the design cover!! You are an amazing artist and I pray you allow the Lord to continue to use your talents for His glory!!

To my pastor and his wife, Steve Hurte and Brenda Ruppe Hurte at Temple Baptist Church—I know you have spent much time praying for not only me but every member of our church. Not only prayer, but hours spent working on sermons; returning texts and answering my questions; time listening to me in prayer group…your wisdom is astounding. I know you would disagree with this, and I also know how you pray for wisdom and discernment—I'm pretty sure you would freely acknowledge your wisdom comes from our Father. Thank you for the time you spend preparing to lead and teach us; thank you for your honesty and your unwavering stand for the Bible and for Jesus. Mrs. Brenda—thank you for teaching me mercy; thank you for the love you have showered on not only me but everyone in our church. Thank you for praying over and for me so many times. Thank you for your Godly example and your wonderful sense of humor. Thank you for acknowledging God in everything you do!!

Contents

Foreword

IN 2020, THE dark days of quarantine for many people began. Covid-19 is a real virus, and it has done tremendous damage worldwide, without a doubt. There are theories about its origins, reality, and power; this book will not address any of those things. Quarantine and Covid are only the inconvenient launching of this book.

I am an ICU nurse, specifically a CVICU nurse. My specialty is taking care of patients immediately after bypass surgery. In my area, we expect sick patients. They are all sick right after bypass surgery; the majority improve rapidly and have amazing outcomes. It is a gratifying, amazing field but it is intense. The scale of Covid-19 upped the ante.

I remember sitting in my recliner feeling torn about even going in to work; the atmosphere with Covid in the hospital had become depressing and oppressive. Quarantine had pushed everyone to a breaking point. I was praying and asking God for one more day of grace and wisdom to keep pushing through.

It was then I felt the first stirrings and inklings of the Holy Spirit prompting me to write a book. Fast forward to 2021 and the medical field is still limping. I'm at home on quarantine again…one of my kids got Covid at camp. Sigh. Again, I felt the prompting…write a book.

I will confess to a big Moses moment. Remember when God called Moses to lead the Israelites out of Egypt and Moses tried to talk God out of it? Exodus 3:11 is his response. "And Moses said unto God, Who am I, that I should go up unto Pharoah, and that I should bring forth the children of Israel out of Egypt?" Who am I, Lord? Me too, Moses. Me too. I'm not planning on bringing a nation out of Egypt, but I surely don't feel especially called to write a book. I do not feel worthy—at all—to write anything for His glory. I am not all that, nor am I the proverbial bag of chips.

My goal is to lift up Jesus. My prayer through this book is to reach one person for Him; to encourage one saint for Him! If it is more, praise His Holy name!! John 12:32 says "And I, if I be lifted up from the earth, will draw all men unto me." These were the words of Jesus. May I humbly lift His name so others may see Him and be reached for Him.

Of note, I will be quoting Scripture throughout this book…heavily and with great emphasis. I will always use the King James Version. I am not debating on any other version of the Bible (there's plenty of resources out there if you want to search or debate); I was raised on the King James Bible and that is what I will be using.

The title of the book sums up my life: I am only here on this earth due to God's amazing, sustaining grace. His grace, mercy, and love have turned me from a victim to a survivor. Without His saving grace, forgiveness, and love I would without a doubt be in hell already or have gone stark raving mad. The confession part? Maybe I should use the term testify—but either one in my mind is accurate. (And it's my book!!) Through this book I am confessing with my mouth the Lord Jesus Christ. He is my Savior, my Redeemer, and He has bestowed more blessings on me than I deserve. My story isn't always pretty, and it's been a bit gut wrenching to put it all on paper, but I feel like it is what God led me to put on paper. Throughout the book I have many personal experiences with grace that I pray will help you!

CHAPTER ONE

Humble Beginnings

WELL, WE ALL have to start somewhere, correct?? Not all of us have wonderful, happy, joyful childhoods. The chapter title should probably hint that my childhood was slightly off center of austere and idyllic.

I am not going to spend a long time detailing specifics of my childhood but what is needed to show the tapestry of how God has worked in my life and show the evidence of His grace. That seems a bit of an oxymoron, correct? I firmly believe there is not one thing in the past, present, or future that my omniscient, omnipresent Abba Father is not in tune with or hasn't used to weave the pattern He wants and needs of any of us. That being said, I am choosing to omit things that could possibly cause pain to anyone I know, love, or am related to. If you ask any person alive on this big, beautiful earth, some person out there somewhere has hurt them; that is the reality of us imperfect humans. I'm not writing this to showcase that hurt; however, I do want to show that God uses those hurts for His glory! There is a tremendous amount of wisdom to that old saying "If you can't say anything nice, don't say anything at all."

I grew up in a small town in Pennsylvania halfway between Philadelphia and beautiful Amish country. I'll give you a hint—I much prefer Amish country! Big cities are loud, bright, and...busy. Not knocking it, but that isn't my overall personality. (Please, don't tell my coworkers this. At work, that pretty much sums me up, especially the loud and busy part!) I do tend to much prefer quiet. My parents both grew up in painful, abusive households and I grew up hearing arguing...loud arguing...lots of arguing...so I tend to retreat into quiet.

My father worked on oil heaters and my mom stayed at home with the kids. My dad, truthfully, was a workaholic and I honestly never got to spend very much time with him. I do have some of his tendencies...I am a very hard worker and stay busy and occupied. He was a big, strong man but tended to be on the silent side. He did have a sense of humor that arose at the strangest and most inappropriate times. While he did accept Jesus as his Savior, he never enjoyed church or being around that many people. One on one, working with his customers, he talked to them, but groups? Not so much. One Christmas, we somehow persuaded him to come to the Christmas program at our church (which was small and since he had worked on the heater there, he knew a few people—bonus!!). Around that time of year, he was always busy. In case no one out there is aware, Pennsylvania tends to be a little chilly in December, and oil heaters break...or need servicing...anyhoo, you get the idea. So, after working 60 hours a week doing repairs and being on call, he was tired. His idea to make folks think he was awake in church? Draw eyeballs on paper and tape them to his glasses. And yes—he did wear them at church and napped straight through the Christmas program!!

My mom wasn't always easy to live with, and on reflection, truthfully, neither was my dad. I honestly believe my dad's workaholic tendencies stemmed from the dual reality of his growing up very poor in rural Maryland with an alcoholic father and avoiding being home. Again, both of my parents grew up poor in terrible homes. My mom's upbringing and the pain caused specifically by her father haunted her throughout her life and definitely impacted her personality and reactions. My mom grew up in a godforsaken hellhole of a home—I don't know how to phrase it any better or "prettier." Mentally and psychologically, she never could escape her past. When I reflect back, I vacillate between feeling she was the weakest person or strongest person ever. Weak (seemingly) because she could never escape the past. She never dealt with it. Now, after living to the ripe old age of 49, there are times I (frighteningly so) totally get some of my mom's responses. Then I think maybe she was one of the strongest people ever.

Mom grew up one of seven, the second born of an unwed couple (which was not looked well on in the 1940's.). Her mom was only 16 when she gave birth to my mom; her first pregnancy was at 12, and my grandfather, who the family aptly named "little Hitler," was at least ten years older. Yes—a 12-year-old girl and a 22-year-old man. One huge gaping question I have always wondered—and WOW could it have changed my family—if the tales were correct (this is my mom's recollections, and I've never researched it; frankly, I'm too horrified) then why on God's green holy earth didn't my grandmother's family separate her from this evil man, who at the very least was guilty of statutory rape? That question remains unanswered. God allowed it; I'm stymied by it. That first pregnancy of my grandmother's was "quietly dealt with"—I'm assuming by a coathanger abortion.

As you can probably guess, abuse was the name of the game with my mother's family. When my mom spoke about her family, it was in a monotone; "just the facts ma'am". No inflection. And for all the horrible details I do know, there was a tremendous amount I don't. I know my mom loved her mother dearly; my grandmother was a severely beaten and psychologically abused woman by my grandfather. Somehow, she managed to love Jesus. Everything related to God my grandfather burned. Bibles, pictures, music—all burned. She was a tiny seed of hope in all the dark.

Moving forward, my parents did not have a match made in heaven. Au contraire: the fights were legendary; my mom's background left her very unstable. She had no trust in my father and wild accusations reigned supreme. My mom had my oldest sister at 17 and my dad married my mom two years later. My second sister took after my mom's side of the family, and I grew up in the throes of full-fledged mental illness between my mom and my sister. My brother was the next child, and I was the youngest. Thankfully, by the time I was born, some of mom's mental instability and cruelty had abated a smidge. But my childhood was, in a word, rough. But here—God's grace. My brother and I have my dad's disposition—you could pretty much run us over with a tank and we will complain, sigh, get up, and get moving again. I am ridiculously thankful for that quality God blessed me with.

I have survived tremendous amounts of abuse. And yes, I do have some emotional scars, as we all have. After years of hearing fighting, I tend not to like arguments. It's probably the closest I will come (aside from a stupid fear of balloons) to a physical reaction; I will shake almost uncontrollably with prolonged arguing. PTSD? Maybe. My second sister, whose name I am leaving out to protect other family, heaped her own psychological, emotional, and physical abuse on the rest of us. And oh, the balloon issue…ahem. That was one of the few times my sister was trying to be nice to me—she rubbed a balloon on my hair to stick it to a wall. Remember that trick? Except that time, it backfired—the balloon popped right next to my ear. Temporarily lost my hearing—just a day or two; but I've been jumpy around balloons ever since. Sigh. Balloons popping, cars backfiring, gunshots…they all elicit the same response in me. I've been the subject of lots of laughter over the years for it!

My dad used to say my sister wasn't "wired right." She spent three years as a teen in and out of mental institutions. I owe her the debt of nearly not being able to pass psych nursing, since at a young age I was dragged into a state mental institution to "visit" her—I was seven or eight at the time. I also have a huge level of distrust thanks to her—honestly her cruelty was so fierce at times that I was afraid to sleep with her in the house. It's very hard for me to admit that. If I had to diagnose her, I would honestly say she was a sociopath.

So where is grace in this lovely family picture?

Grace comes in God using sometimes the most terrible circumstances to draw people to Him. You see, I was sent to a Christian school because of how my sister acted. My mom could not deal with the thought of having another child who behaved like her—so my brother and I were sent to Christian school. So would I have gotten saved if it weren't for her? I don't know. What I DO know is God used her to lead me to Him. One thing my mom did absolutely right—after trying to raise her and seeing how badly her self-destructive behavior destroyed her, my mom was determined not to let her other two kids (my brother and I) follow my sister's path. The truth? As a teen I resented the constant "no you can't do that because you'll end up like her" comparisons; the constant denigrating distrust my mother had when I became "pretty" at age 16 (my sister was gorgeous and she used those looks to ensnare a lot of men); BUT I know in my heart that even though her methods were not the best, she did have good intentions and wanted to protect me from the near legendary poor decision making skills of my sister.

Grace comes in my having that big ol' weakness—remember the balloon? Silly thing, but I don't laugh at people who have phobias. I don't make them feel bad about it—I'll happily come pick up your rat/snake/spider/mouse/bat, and I'll take it outside without a word. Doesn't sound much like grace—until you're the person terrified of something, and people are making fun of you. I'll be that person off to the side quietly telling you it'll be ok and hopefully letting you breathe normal again. In this case—humans can extend grace to each other!!

OK, who remembers Joseph in the Bible? Sort of a similar but different thing here. One huge thing—what was meant for evil God used for good. God used my sister, in a strange way, to lead me to Him. So many things, looking back, where despite the horrible pain and awful fear of my childhood, I can see His hand of protection. I see the tapestry He wove, where my side sure looked awful, but His side was a totally different pattern! My heart hurts knowing with fair certainty that she is not spending eternity in heaven, unless she accepted Christ at the last minute as the drugs she took to kill herself ended her life. After a lifetime of suicide attempts, mental institutions, and who knows the pain she inflicted on herself and others, she ended her own life at age 46. She had suffered terrible pain herself after multiple car accidents and back and neck surgeries; I can attest to the fact that chronic pain does awful things to the mind. One of my many regrets in life is even though I forgave her for so many wrongs, I never told her that. Would anything have changed if I had reached out to her and ended two years of not speaking to each other? I don't know. What I will encourage you, my friends reading this, is try your best to breach gaps. I can tell you working in healthcare you never know when that last time you talk to someone is.

My oldest sister, my half-sister technically, did a lot to help raise me—she was 11 years older than me, and my second sister (just mentioned) was quite obviously giving my parents a hard time, to put it mildly. I have her to thank for teaching me my alphabet at an early age, reading young, and the love of crochet!! She taught me to crochet at age six. There were many years of our lives we were separated, unfortunately; I am thankful that we are talking now and that she is now a Christian!! Another amazing example of God's grace and timing! She is also an encouragement: do not stop praying for those you love to accept Jesus Christ as their Savior!! Never quit bringing them to God! Never stop praying for God to use an opportunity to draw people to Him. Keep inviting people to church. Text, call, or write to that person who God is prompting you to!!

My brother and I are the closest in age, closest in temperament— we were twins separated by four years. We both have the same political leanings, the same warped sense of humor, sarcasm, etc. We even look eerily similar, but I think I've aged better. Ha!! We had some fights as kids—as we both got bigger and physically stronger, the competition changed; even simple ping pong games were a good-natured source of pseudo friendly competition. (Did you know you can break a ping pong ball in half if you hit it hard enough?? Now you do…) Being the closest in age, I don't know if my childhood would have been survivable without him. I don't tell him this enough, but he was a rock. He was absolutely an instrument of God's grace! We didn't have long talks about what was occurring in the family, but we had a "silent solidarity" in each other. He defended me to my mom when she assumed the worst in me in her paranoia. He was and still is excellent at defusing volatile situations; that's something we are both good at—we are peacemakers. Is he perfect? Ummmmm…no. Far from it. I'm so thankful and grateful that God in His mercy and grace provided me with a sibling close in age that had a similar temperament; that has the personality to calm and defuse; that served as a solid rock against volatility and at times near madness.

Point of reflection: can you think of a time in your past, be it your childhood or just earlier in life—anytime in life, really—where you can clearly recognize in retrospect God was working and moving? Can you think of a time when someone meant evil for you and God used it for good?

To go with this, I think of one of my favorite verses here—Jeremiah 29:11. "For I know the thoughts I think toward you, saith the Lord, thoughts of peace, and not of evil, to give you an expected end." This verse sprung to mind immediately. Even though I experienced so much evil during my childhood, it wasn't God thinking those thoughts; He used that evil for my good. Have I still questioned many times? Yup— God forgive me, sometimes on the daily. But that is where FAITH comes in—believe that even though we can't see good in our circumstances, know that He can work good!

CHAPTER TWO

Reye's Syndrome

I CAN'T ESCAPE talking about my early childhood without telling of a pivotal time in my life. As a child, I was healthy but overweight—not morbidly so, just a little on the "husky/heavy" side. Honestly, I've struggled with my weight all my life. However, every winter, being cooped up indoors in the cold Pennsylvania winters and being exposed to my parents' heavy smoking and wood burning stove, I always ended up with a bad winter cold (now I know it was probably sinus infections, but back in my day it was a cold and you'd be fine. Apparently, they were right??). December 1979 through January 1980 was no different.

In December I got the flu over Christmas break. I remember laying on the couch drinking hot tea and eating toast for days. (Can I get a witness??) In January, the chicken pox decided to visit. Now, like it or lump it, in those days you had chicken pox parties and "got it over with." This wasn't my case—I just got them. Anyhoo. Here's my oddity (I assure you the first of many!)—on retrospective study (I'm a nerd without apology), no one put together that every time I had to chew and swallow those hideously nasty St. Joseph's baby aspirin, I always threw them back up—

with change. No one realized that honestly, I was allergic to aspirin. Even now, I can't eat an orange creamsicle because of those stupid things! Any form or derivative of aspirin makes me sick. Even if it gets on my skin, it causes me to break out in a rash. I'm so much fun to shop for skin care products for!!

Well, that fateful January, having chicken pox covering my entire slightly weakened body (bear in mind I had just gotten over the flu), my mom gave me baby aspirin. In her defense, they didn't have children's Tylenol yet, so she had nothing else to give me for the high fever I had developed. This one time, those stupid aspirin stayed down. The only time!! So I fell asleep—but after 24 hours, when my mom couldn't awaken me, she knew something was wrong. Turns out there is a specific interaction between aspirin and chicken pox called Reye's syndrome and I had developed it. It is an inflammation of the liver (hepatitis) and the brain (encephalitis). This form of hepatitis is a true inflammation and not infectious like other forms.

So where, you might be asking, is grace in this story?

Stepping back a bit—let me add, dwelling on the past is not needful and sometimes is very harmful. I don't think it's healthy to dwell on and relive trauma over and over again. Don't waste time reliving hard and horrible events! DO take the time to recognize the hand of God in your past!! At seven and a half years old, I sure didn't recognize God working—I wasn't even saved yet!!

Back to the story (ahem)—as it would happen, the month before my mom had read about this condition in the Reader's Digest (I loved those magazines!). She remembered reading the symptoms, recognized them, and knew to call my pediatrician. Friends, there are no "just so happened" moments with God—He is working, moving; His hands are always busy! The pediatrician told my mom to get me to his office and from there I was taken by ambulance to Children's Hospital of Philadelphia. Without the hand of God working even then in the lives of lost people, I wouldn't be here today boring the snot out of all of you!

A quick Google search gave me some numbers on Reye's syndrome. Just to show you how unique I am, in 1980 there was a peak number of 555 cases of Reye's syndrome in the United States. (1) Since then, there have been no more than 36 cases per year. The initial mortality rate was 60 percent, but now with supportive care it is around 20 percent. (In other words, back then 60 percent of people who had this complication died.) My pediatrician told my mom after I had recovered that I was his first survivor. Now you ask—why does this even matter? First of all, I had no clue there were that few cases. I was astonished by this. I honestly thought it was pretty common back then. Second, and more importantly actually, I was seven and a half when I developed this. I didn't ask Jesus to save me until I was ten years old, in fifth grade!! If I had not survived, I would have been in hell. God protected me, without a shadow of a doubt!! Third, I have no residuals from this. None! God not only allowed me to survive an incredibly rare childhood illness, but He restored me to complete health! I am sure my parents agonized over it; I honestly don't remember much of anything.

I do have a few blips of memories from that time, however. Truthfully, I didn't talk to my mom very much about it—in my family, we didn't talk through hard times, we tended to bury 'em deep and hope for the best, so things are limited. I remember waking up very briefly in my pediatrician's den—his office was in the front part of his house. My mind registered a quick "snapshot" photo in my head. I remember the rough tweed couch (remember those from the 70's?), the brown shag carpet, and bookcases. The next "flash" of memory was in the ambulance on the way to the hospital. I saw the paramedic. Just for a second. But I saw his face, and weirdly enough I recognized him later! The next time I woke up I was in the hospital. I'm guessing this was day two of my being there. I'm told I was semi-comatose for three days. I remember putting my hand on my head, feeling something, and then falling back to sleep. Being a nurse and knowing how we monitor brain waves and activity;

I'm assuming those were those super annoying EEG leads but it could have been any electronic leads.

I fully awakened on day three in the hospital. I remember seeing my mom holding my stuffed Rudolph toy. I loved that toy! He was weighted at the bottom and his red nose was slightly brown from when he had tried to "help" me drink hot chocolate. Oops!! Sadly, with my childhood, I remember being surprised that she was there. My mom hated hospitals. There were things she just had a hard time conquering, like we all do. Sometimes it's awfully hard to remember we are "more than conquerors through him that loved us" (Romans 8:37). I don't remember anything she said; she gave me my Rudolph toy. I was very tired and sleepy that day; we were sent home from the hospital not long afterwards. The only treatment I remember after the Reye's was being packed up every Saturday morning and being taken to the hospital to get labs drawn—week after week—for months. Again, referring to my own nurse and lab experience, I'm fairly certain they were checking my liver enzymes to ensure they had normalized. I have NO long-term liver damage. Ain't that some grace??

This might all seem like "wow that's a crazy story" stuff to you, but I've done some research on Reye's and talked to my doc friends about it, and I know for sure the mighty hand of God in His grace surely protected my immune system!! After I recovered from Reye's and chicken pox, I got very sick—again—with some terrible bronchitis. No, not hospital sick—praise Jesus!! Just sick enough to miss more school. I'm guessing I missed over a month of school that winter. I was in second grade at the time, and all of this occurred with my dear second grade teacher, who I'll introduce you to in the next chapter. She played a pivotal role in my spiritual life.

Point of reflection: at any point, have you survived what could or should have been a fatal illness, car accident, etc? I know many people in our COVID era who, in reality, should have died—but I also think of many heart attack and heart surgery survivors, cancer survivors, car accident survivors, etc who should have died as well. What did God teach you or show you during or about that time?

I think of Philippians 3:10 here. "That I may know him (Jesus), and the power of his resurrection, and the fellowship of his sufferings, being made comformable unto his death." Odd verse to choose? I actually had a different verse written down, but God gave me this one instead. As hard as sickness and pain are, there is a depth to knowing God, learning about God, and getting close to God that truly is only known during suffering. I also think of Matthew 10:30—"But the very hairs of your head are all numbered." What comfort—He knows us down to the smallest detail that we brush out! Our time on this earth is already known to the second by our Father!

CHAPTER THREE

The Beginning of my Journey to God

I WANT TO begin this chapter by mentioning that I do not believe AT ALL in coincidences. I believe wholeheartedly in the providence and workings of a living, loving God. I also believe He uses people to accomplish His work. I did a Bible study during quarantine last year (I know—quarantine—hiss and spit!! How could anything good come from that mess??) and a large focus was on obeying God. If we love God, we will obey God, just as a sign of love to our earthly parents is obedience. I am so very imperfect with this, but it was an eye-opening study. God worked HARD on my heart in my struggle with obedience. (Wait…WHAT?) Yes…I struggle. Not in the typical way—I'm a pretty decent "rule follower", but what I struggle with more is yielding my heart to His will and listening to Him: trying to actively focus when God is trying to direct me. I also struggled mightily prior to this study with fully accepting the love of God for me—being raised in the family I was in precluded me to being hesitant and almost untrusting of love and very much feeling unworthy of any love. More on that topic later.

My second-grade teacher, whose name I will not mention (she has since passed on—I look forward one day to giving her a big hug in heaven!!), seemed to do better with this than I do, thankfully! This was the grade I was in during my roughly two-month long bout of illnesses. This dear saint of a teacher and saint of God brought papers to the house so I wouldn't fall behind; brought homemade cards from my classmates, and most importantly she invited a sickly, lonely little girl to church. Now, to be fair, I had gone to church a rare handful of times. I knew (sort of!) what Christmas was about. I had even, at age five, prayed a prayer—I do not think at that time I understood what I was praying and don't believe I was saved at that time.

We began, at her invitation, attending a small, independent Bible believing church. They had a bus ministry, thankfully—at the time my mom didn't drive, and my dad wasn't at all interested in church. I don't recall him ever having malice towards the church, merely disinterest. My mom at that time was very suspicious, bordering on paranoid, with most people—my middle sister was wreaking havoc at home, getting arrested, running away from home—and I honestly believe my mom was completely overwhelmed. She cut off our family from the rest of her family and my dad's family during this time and we really only spent time with her best friend and her family. During my childhood my mom suffered from horrible depression—her first suicide attempt that I remember was when I was 8. I wish she had accepted Jesus earlier and had been able, by grace, to heal—but the time would come.

My brother and I would get on the church bus and go to Sunday school and church. I remember learning some songs and some Bible stories—I don't have any clear memories or recall of a couple years of my childhood. There was a significant amount of trauma surrounding that time; I will spare you a few of the ugly things I do remember, and instead reiterate—even NOT remembering is a testimony of grace. But how?

Could I process the trauma? Clearly my mind couldn't. However, I can tell you with absolute assurance that it is a mercy of God that I do not recall some times. I will gladly take that instead of the constant rewind in my brain. God indeed knows me better than I know myself, and He is well aware of my limitations. He answered my prayers removing those memories from me!

My sister's behavior worsened, prompting my mom to enroll my brother and I in Christian school. I started at my first Christian school in fourth grade and my brother was in eighth grade. She hadn't really even started attending church herself, but the kindness of the people at my church had to have softened my mom's heart! And here is one point I want to drive home: if my second-grade teacher and the sweet people at my first church hadn't obeyed God's calling to talk to me and invite us to church, where would I be today? If God is calling you to talk to someone, DO IT. We are called to be the hands and feet of Jesus! We are all part of the body of Christ—some of us are called to be those hands and feet, some the mouth, etc—but we are all called to work together. I encourage you, friends—if God is prompting you to do something, to encourage someone, call someone—whatever it is, DO IT. As a person who has dealt with pain and feeling unworthy, unloved, and forgotten many times, I am sensitive to that and try my best to encourage and reach out to people. Be that person who encourages and edifies. Be that person who tells someone they are doing well! Be that person who sends a text or message and lets them know you're thinking of them.

In fifth grade, I have a clear recollection of a special Christmas concert called "Ring the Bells". At the end of the program, they gave an invitation, and I remember walking up that aisle with a recent friend. Her name was Katrina, as I recall, and I remain thankful to the kindness and acceptance she showed to a little girl who was unaccepted. I do not recall exactly what I prayed that night; I wish I remembered the date! But this memory, so crystal clear, was another evidence of grace from God—both in salvation and memory. This was still in the block of time when I have nothing but fleeting memories, and I remember in my adult years, struggling with remembering a "moment of salvation," and God allowed me to recognize when this memory was. When my poor brain finally realized what a gift this was, when my brain was essentially a blank canvas for a couple of years—oh what a moment. That God should show so much caring and love to open the fog and allow such a memory to be etched in! I remain so thankful and grateful. I remember crying in my room when it struck me that God had preserved this clear memory of that time.

I never, during my childhood after salvation, felt like any kind of spiritual giant. I was never a "bad" kid. I had seen what my sister's behavior and poor choices led to and I recognized that she had nothing but bad outcomes. The imprinting of why her choices and behavior was bad was never explained. My entire childhood was really spent trying to fly under my mom's radar—any attention paid was negative. I became adept at doing my best to fly in the middle yet still be "good enough" in my mom's eyes. Throughout my high school years those feelings didn't change. I did, however, finally learn the why's of poor choices and the Biblical reasons behind what made sin a sin.

My friend, have you ever struggled with feeling completely unworthy and unlovable? May I confess, I have plenty of days that I still feel that way. Then I purpose that I will keep remembering, purposefully, that I am a chosen, blood bought child of the King!! One of the weird things that I wish hadn't happened in second grade was my teacher recognizing that I was ahead of the curve with learning. I learned to read at a very early age—I was reading fifth grade books in kindergarten and first grade, and that was normal to me. She encouraged my mom to have my IQ tested and have me placed in gifted classes. How is that bad, you ask? Well, from that point forward I wasn't allowed to get a B—after all, I had an IQ of 145. (Big fat hairy honking deal—I have a good memory. Yay!) (Although that memory has come in weirdly handy writing this book, but I digress…) So B's weren't good enough. It was all A's or bust. And if I could get A's, why not A+'s? I think you get the idea. Between that and the constant drumming in my head that I was "fat", I never felt like I measured up. But God in His grace kept on me…grace is FREE, it is a gift, and it has nothing to do with my merit! Once I finally got ahold of that, oh what freedom!!

My time in high school, spiritually, felt like driftwood overall. I struggled to feel some level of acceptance, just like many high school kids. I finally felt some level when I started playing volleyball—honestly when I started playing, I probably looked like a giraffe in high heels stumbling around, but during eighth grade and ninth grade something started clicking. In seventh grade I grew six inches in five months and my "baby fat" finally stretched itself out. Ha! Suddenly I was 5'8" in eighth grade—by the time I graduated high school I was 5'10" and in college I added another inch. I got more aggressive about diving. I practiced at home. I remember doing 200 sit-ups and 100 pushups a day. I never had to stretch—I was ridiculously flexible (that has come back to haunt me but it sure was handy then!), earning the nickname Gumby. I managed to ignore the pain of landing on the hardwood floors. Honestly, I know in retrospect I was grasping at anything to escape the reality of home and the pressure of home. I learned to hit the ball harder. And honestly there was so much catharsis in being to let off any steam. Did it help my spiritual life? Really, it became another god during the season. I wanted to play so bad; God allowed it. Truly, I learned so many "life lessons" about hard work, shaking off pain, teamwork, and responsibility during my five years playing JV and varsity volleyball but I do regret how much precedence it took.

One of my biggest character flaws is my ability to stay endlessly busy and to multitask. How is this bad? I keep myself busy many times to not allow time for introspection, prayer, and Bible reading. OK—one of many secrets out. Why do I do this? Truthfully, after the past couple years working through this, it's because I tend to hold people at arm's length— even tried that with God. If I share my deep, really deep, secrets with someone there is such vulnerability I tend to feel that I will be judged or pitied—neither option is good. So, the emotional walls tend to stay up. But again, God in His amazing grace—I think of the book of Hosea, where God commanded Hosea to marry a prostitute and then had him go back again and woo her AGAIN despite her walking away—this is how God is. We want to pull away from Him and He wants us to draw near to Him. I sympathize with Gomer, Hosea's wife—not in the sense of her prostitution, but the lack of trust and pulling away. Volleyball, crocheting, reading, and a bunch of other things in an endless list of "stuff" so many times have allowed me to try to keep God at a bit of arm's length. I'm so thankful, so grateful He keeps pursuing and pulling things away from me to keep me focused on Him.

Why, you may ask, did I include this last paragraph right here? Well, again—it's my book, not yours, so…OK, just kidding. I've had years to reflect back on bad and good choices. Was volleyball or any other sport I played a bad choice? Not necessarily. My motives initially weren't bad—I just wanted to try to play and be involved. That morphed into a super competitive inner drive to be faster, stronger, and better. I was still replacing something very temporal when I needed an eternal solution. We all do this. Feeling down? Go shopping, get a coffee, go for a walk, find a friend—are any of these sinful? No. Will they necessarily fix what ails us? Not really. They are all temporary band aids. (But that pumpkin pie coffee I had earlier sure was a tasty band aid! OK, I'm done…)

So where does grace come in during this time?

I've mentioned a few already but I'll mention them again…

The biggest example was my salvation and actually recalling it. What a gift of grace! And it is indeed by grace we are saved through faith! (Ephesians 2:8). I see a huge thread of grace, unmerited favor, woven through all along my sister's path—I see God's protection in keeping me safe at the mental institution; His mercy and grace allowing me to choose sports over Him many times without my coming to harm. Grace in allowing me to have a good memory to learn, but even MORE grace sometimes allowing me to forget. I see mercy and grace together in the couple of times I cheated. (Believe it or not, one time to finish an Awana book—a kid's Bible book!) While I asked forgiveness of God for those times, I never tried to rectify those couple of times; the folks involved have since passed and ironically, the trophy I earned partially through cheating God allowed later to be destroyed—more on that later! I would love to say I could justify the cheating because I knew my mom would rip me a new one if I didn't finish; if I didn't get an A on that test despite my parents keeping me awake all hours of the night with screaming arguments—all in all, maybe it is justified in my mind, but it is still a sin.

I see grace in His protection in so many ways.

I see mercy in sparing me from the consequences of some actions, and grace in His blessing me anyway—WOW. Do you realize, my friend, truly what God has protected you from? I challenge you one day to make a list acknowledging God's mercy and grace just in what you know about. How about the many times God protected you and you won't have a clue about until we see Jesus face to face in heaven? He is always working! Romans 8:28 says "And we know that all things work together for good to them that love God, to them who are the called according to his purpose." That whole "work together for good" phrase has, at times, felt like an oxymoron when I'm at a time where it doesn't feel the least bit "good." Our good doesn't mean a big house, fancy car—maybe God will gift us that, but the good here is making me more like Jesus. That is good, and sometimes that good doesn't feel at all good. High school didn't feel "good" to me the bulk of the time. That's the time to choose faith, choose to keep following Him, and hang on.

I've left this chapter sitting for two days. I haven't felt like this chapter was finished yet, but I debated putting this next tidbit in here. But after all, I can't just focus on what I've gone through either by circumstances or what I dealt with due to other people's actions without including a big moment in childhood where my own rank stupidity and poor decision-making skills (OK, let's just call it sin, folks—because it was, no matter how hard I try to justify it!) even then became a testimony or grace. Show of hands—has anyone else had that happen? Just me?

So, here is one of my pretty epic fails in life. Remember back a while ago mentioning my sister running away from home? She ran away at 13, 14, and 16—and 16 was the last straw for my mom. She kicked her out. Threw her stuff out the bedroom window and onto the lawn. Yup. Well, I turned 16. I FINALLY had a guy ask me out. Go me!! My mom promised at 16 I could date. When he asked, she told me no—there was always a "reason;" this was he had a mullet. (It was 1988—everyone had a mullet!! HA!) Well, we snuck around and met places, thanks to my childhood best friend covering for me. Her house, the youth center on Saturday nights (it actually was a Christian activity center—they played a Christian based movie and then had various activities set up. It was cool!). Really, honestly? Acceptable dates for a Christian girl—if I wasn't sneaking and being disobedient. My mom found out (all moms do, we are amazing that way), and I got "you're going to end up like your sister" or, he just wants you in bed—GASP!! My mom actually said that to me? Bear in mind, her first child was out of wedlock, and she had already seen my sister make those mistakes…and well, worse was said too.

Over the course of a couple of weeks, I was able to talk to this guy on the phone and a couple times met him somewhere and my mom seemed ok with it. He worked at a local grocery store and I'm guessing since I would talk to him in broad daylight in front of my mom and he was polite to her, it seemed to soften her. Well, you can guess what happened next—eventually we snuck away somewhere, and we kissed. That was IT—nothing more. In no way am I saying it's not a big deal, because there is definitely an intimacy in kissing; barriers are broken! My mom found out and she was relentless. The fights were constant. I was constantly belittled, criticized, and compared to my sister. And ya know what? None of that justifies what I did, but in my mind it did.

I was so desperate for a little freedom, a chance at normalcy, love and acceptance, LIFE. I felt like I had no freedom, no resources, no one to turn to. Again, I was a Christian, but I had gotten pretty good at pushing God away and looking to someone else for help. At that time, I honestly didn't know of one person I could talk to who I felt would listen to me. In reality, that wasn't true—the devil kept me too scared to reach out to anyone. Fear is a HORRIBLE tool he uses, and he is good with it. Praise Jesus, I've figured out by now that things don't work out well to keep God out of the equation! I was mentally abandoned in a morass of helplessness. In my family, we tend to go to our separate corners and lick our wounds privately. There was no point in attempting to communicate with my mom—it wouldn't have helped. She tended to scorn others' emotions and there were no open discussions, at least not until I got into my twenties. So...faced with a decision to make, neither one of which was good at all, I ran away. My other alternative was drinking the two bottles of nail polish remover I had in my room, and frankly I doubted its ability to do the job. (We didn't have any aspirin in the house anymore—ok, bad joke.) So, I ran away.

I walked to a neighbor's house down the road first, where a nice unsuspecting lady allowed me to use her phone. I called this guy I had been "seeing;" he said he would be there to pick me up. I told this sweet lady my mom was abusive, and I had to get away. She asked if we needed the police and I said no. I was 16 but looked to be in my early twenties. She let me hide in her house. I remember seeing my mom drive up the road in her '55 Chevy, by this point knowing I was gone, but not where I was. I almost chose to reveal myself but didn't.

My guy friend picked me up. Initially, since I had all my cash with me from my first job, I wanted him to take me to the airport, but I realized I needed to plan more first. The end goal? I wanted to fly to South Carolina where my now sister-in-law was going to Bible college at Bob Jones. Instead, I asked him to take me to my best friend's house. Her parents knew how hard things were at my parents' house, from my perspective. Truthfully, if anything I buried many problems. Because of my mom's many issues, very rarely was she seen at school; my dad was never at my school. I was moody, irritated, and angry most of my teen years. Her parents didn't call my mom, but my mom figured out that I had to have gone to her house. When she and my brother showed up a couple hours later, I knew my proverbial goose was cooked.

What followed next at my pastor's house was…rough. My mom interrogated me and glared at me with her Ukrainian death glare. Laugh if you want, but to this day I can feel her loathing and near hatred in that glare. My pastor's wife tried to defend me—she tried to help. The betrayal I felt the worst was from my brother. I felt so alone because he never defended me. When I asked him later, he said he couldn't let mom get "hung out to dry" alone. Did I forgive him eventually? Yes. Trust was broken in me that day, though—what could have been a time of reconciliation ended up being a deeper divide, and my mom's trust in me was for good reason destroyed.

So where, you ask, does grace come in here??

Where is the good?

Because—in spite of my awful decisions and actions, God worked for my good. Crazy, weird stuff.

My best friend knew of an opening at the Christian camp where she worked at in the summer in the kitchen. Somehow, between my pastor and her father (also a pastor), I was allowed to work there for the summer.

I had a summer without my mom's constant oppression, mistrust, and loathing.

I had (some) freedom.

But I learned responsibility and accountability.

And I STILL messed up and sinned there. (One day I'll learn—but apparently not at 16….)

I learned to cook. And I had adults who every day invested in me in some way, either big or small. They kept me in line and on the straight and narrow—they didn't accept my excuses but with love and explaining, so much explaining, made me realize how wrong my actions were and helped me in tremendous ways.

Honestly, it was the highlight of my childhood/teen years aside from playing volleyball—and it was proof—looking back—that even when we sin, God can somehow, in some way, work out a way of escape.

That cooking thing? Yeah. I still use that—a lot. I mean, a lot a lot. I've had to. Would I have learned how otherwise? Maybe. But that summer, God put adults in my life—consistent adults, not rare visitors—who every day invested in this kid who was love starved and seeking. Searching for acceptance in whatever form—eventually at camp even drawing closer to God.

It wasn't the right way; I have long since acknowledged and confessed that sin. I confessed it to both God and my mom and asked for forgiveness. Unfortunately, even with my sincerity, it took years to rebuild my mom's trust—and understandably so. My choices of colleges were limited to one because of it. I got compared to my sister. But I also learned to be more internally quiet, to rationalize better, and to make way better choices. I learned about trust and broken trust. And finally, I started to really learn to pray and spend more time with God. Most importantly for me at that time, I finally realized I was never alone—the God of all creation had never left me.

I Peter 5:5b—"God resisteth the proud, and giveth grace to the humble." Boy howdy, did I get a massive dose of humble pie with this experience. And I needed it. Even more so I was showered in His grace. God protected me from stupid, horrible choices. He allowed me to get a glimpse of something (cooking) that He knew I would need later and absolutely love. He allowed wonderful, loving adults into my life; people that I would look back on how they handled things positively. That's my God!!

Before I end this really super difficult to write chapter, I feel compelled to share some humor. I love to laugh and laugh big; and I feel like I've painted my mom as this terrible monster—but she wasn't always that way. So let me share some good stuff.

I figured out as a pretty young kid how to defuse my mom's temper—laughter. I got really good at it. Stupid stuff—slapstick humor. She loved Johnny Carson on the Tonight Show (yes, I am that old!). Loved impromptu. Growing up around farm country in Pennsylvania, we saw unusual meats used commonly—like, say, cow tongue (we actually call it sweet bread up there—talk about a weird confusing name!). We would go to the grocery store, and I would go to the meat case and grab a cow tongue (don't worry, they're very well packaged!) and sneak up behind her and make it lick her cheek. Cracked her up every time. Or we would go to the store, and I would grab a Toblerone candy bar and use it as a microphone.

"Ma'am, what do you think of your daughter today?" She never could answer—she would be laughing too hard at my idiocy.

We would stand there reading greeting cards in the drugstore, passing each other funny cards to read, gasping and wheezing with laughter. I miss those times with my mom. Oh, how she struggled with mental illness for years and the agony she lived with in her mind. I'm so thankful God in His grace gave me the gift of humor and the wisdom to know when to throw some out to defuse my mom. My mom accepted Jesus as her Savior when I was 12 and she was 40—I wish she had come to know Him sooner, and I wish she had learned to lean on Him more fully, but I understand, finally, why it was such a struggle for her. She changed so much after she got saved, she really did—but she never could fully let go of the past.

I love crying and praising God; hands raised listening to gospel music; that "right song at the right time" moment that God will use. On the flip side, I also love laughing until I can't breathe, tears streaming down my face moments where you've had a 20-minute ab session, too. Life was awfully hard on me sometimes as a kid—I'll never deny that, but I'm so thankful for those moments of life, laughter, and joy.

Point of reflection: have you ever at this point in time accepted God's free gift of salvation? Have you experienced His grace and mercy firsthand? Are you in a spot now that you've walked away from Him, and you need a renewing of your Christian faith? My friend, I encourage you—beg you even—turn to God or find your way back to God! He is as close as your first step toward Him. I promise you; the things of this world will eventually not satisfy you. Find a friend, a mentor—someone who knows Jesus—and get your questions answered. Find a Bible and READ IT. Keep reading and keep digging. Pray like you've never prayed before. He is WORTH IT!!

II Corinthians 6:2—"(For he saith, I have heard thee in a time accepted, and in the day of salvation have I succoured thee: behold, now is the accepted time; behold, now is the day of salvation.)"

Not one of us is guaranteed tomorrow—don't hesitate, don't wait to turn back to Him!!

CHAPTER FOUR

What is this thing called "Grace?"

GRACE IS A central concept of Christianity; others I think of are mercy, forgiveness, and love. There are many other important concepts, of course, but in my limited and finite opinion these four stand out the most. When I think of the holy God of Scripture, these come to mind first, although holy and healer are two more that come to mind.

So, what exactly is grace? The dictionary definitions of grace are quite varied, but some of them, according to Merriam-Webster (2), include unmerited divine assistance given to humans for their regeneration or sanctification. Others include mercy or pardon, privilege, a temporary exemption (reprieve), the quality or state of being considerate or thoughtful. In Hebrew, grace literally means "favour;" "chem" from the root word "chanon," meaning to bend or stoop in kindness to another as a superior to an inferior (3). Charis is the Greek form of the word grace; it is also spelled Karis (personal shoutout to my niece Grace Charis—grace on grace!!).

That Hebrew meaning of grace, though—I can't quite get beyond that. If that is not a picture of our loving heavenly Father reaching out to us, over and over again, to soften a blow; offer a safe place to land (in my mind I just picture an enveloping recliner and soft pillow!); offering a heavenly "hand up." And it makes me picture a parent bending down and offering a hand to their child who had just fallen. Oh my…how our Father, in His perfection and holiness, does this for us! How often do I fail to extend that grace to others around me? God forgive me…

I also can't get away from this section without mentioning how much music means to me—every person is different; how we worship is different, how God touches us and helps us is as unique as we are, but for me, gospel music has been a way God has helped me for as long as I can remember.

Growing up, music has always been huge for me—I love to sing (not solos, but I can rock out that joyful noise thing) and I've sung in choirs since elementary school. Listening to music definitely soothes my soul.

That being said, I'll be including a few songs in this book—I've had the privilege of meeting some gospel music artists and two of them have graciously allowed me to use their songs in this book. The ones I have met are so kind and caring and you feel like you're friends the minute you meet them. Hearing their testimonies had an influence on this book. One of my favorites, Joseph Habedank, has a tremendous testimony. He also writes a great deal of his own music and has got an amazing voice. It carries across how personal the songs are to him. I am sure that if he wanted to, he could be singing any kind of music on any kind of stage and making money hand over fist, but he chooses to use his music and testimony to draw people to God and help others. This first song, "This Grace," is on his Deeper Oceans CD (4). I love the words:

I once stood as a sworn enemy of the God who kept pouring out kindness;

I once stood with an angry clenched fist till He whispered and silenced my fightings.

Undone, undone—I could not escape it!

Ten thousand times I could sing it; there's ten thousand ways I've received it!

It never runs out, it never grows cold!

Just when I thought I'd reached the limit, it keeps pouring out—I'm drowning in it!

It won't shut me out, it won't let me go

So I'll keep singing on and on of this grace, I'll keep singing on and on of this grace—I'll keep singing on.

Some may say that it's foolish, but how could you ever grow tired of such goodness?

I just know that I must sing, I won't see a drop of His grace ever wasted!

Undone, undone—I cannot escape it!

Ten thousand times I could sing it, there's ten thousand ways I've received it

It never runs out, it never grows cold!

Just when I thought I'd reached the limit, it keeps pouring out—I'm drowning in it!

It won't shut me out, it won't let me go

So I'll keep singing on and on of this grace; I'll keep singing on and on of this grace, I'll keep singing on and on of this grace—I'll keep singing on!

I've got so many songs I could include just in this chapter, but I won't—for sheer length of the book alone, honestly! I am so incredibly thankful for the church I am at now and I've been at for the past 20 years—one of the things that drew me to it was the earnestness of worship I saw in the choir. I am SO incredibly blessed to be there and humbled to be a part of that worship now. Are we perfect? No. Just my walking in the door ensures we are not—ha!! We sure do recognize grace in there and we sure do love Jesus!!

I asked some of my friends, who shall remain anonymous, what their personal definition of grace is. My personal definition is an unanticipated, often unasked for and sometimes unrecognized gift from God—in my own case, especially in the writing of this book, I can look back and see just how many times God has showered grace on me that I didn't see until I started looking for it. Here are the other definitions:

Unexpected and undeserved gift given in the form of love

Free, undeserved, gift given in the form of love

Receiving pardon for something you shouldn't be pardoned for

Loving someone despite their mistakes

Giving something to someone when they don't deserve it; compassion

Unmerited favor; the acrostic "God's Riches At Christ's Expense"

The Lord generously using what could be a discipline lesson as a teaching lesson for my heart

Allowance for error with a smidge of or sometimes a ton of compassion

God's unmerited favor

Even when we sin, God's love being great enough to still show us kindness

I LOVE all of these definitions—I can see the personal highlights of them! When I think of grace, I also think of mercy. I will borrow the oft repeated "mercy is God not giving us what we do deserve, grace is God giving us what we don't deserve." (I haven't been able to find the original source of this quote!) Instead of eternal punishment or damnation, God gives forgiveness and an eternity with Him once we accept His Son Jesus as the Savior of our lives and souls! He is the only way to obtain forgiveness from our sins! He indeed paid it all!

Instead of a lifetime of toil, trouble, and unending struggle, as Christians, we have an unlimited and often untapped source of help from a very willing God Who wants us to bring our burdens to Him! In Matthew 11:28-30 Jesus says, "Come unto me, all ye that labour and are heavy laden, and I will give you rest. Take my yoke upon you, and learn of me; for I am meek and lowly in heart: and ye shall find rest unto your souls. For my yoke is easy, and my burden is light." I can't recall how many times my stubborn, headstrong self either consciously or subconsciously thought I could absolutely do something by myself when I have the source of all strength to call on!

My pastor sent me a link that had some excellent points about grace. The website was gotquestions.org (5). I am going to summarize a few points off of it that I hadn't pondered before. What is it that makes grace so important? Grace is a gift freely given; it costs the giver but is totally free to the recipient! In the Bible our salvation is by grace through faith (Ephesians 2:8-9), but the grace we experience at salvation doesn't stop there! It is a lifelong, unending, ever pouring gift from God. It is intangible, but to those who have experienced grace we can testify beyond a shadow of a doubt of its reality! We cannot "pay back" grace. All we are able to do is extend the grace God gives us to others!

Point of reflection: Can you name a time or place in your life and see where grace played a major, pivotal role? Can you reflect back on it and keep it in your remembrance, so when doubts come (and they will!!) you can combat those doubts? When Satan tries to convince you God doesn't care, no one cares—you have to have a way to fight back.

Ephesians 6:11-18—"Put on the whole armour of God, that ye may be able to stand against the wiles of the devil. For we wrestle not against flesh and blood, but against principalities, against powers, against the rulers of the darkness of this world, against spiritual wickedness in high places. Wherefore take unto you the whole armour of God, that we may be able to withstand in the evil day, and having done all, to stand. Stand therefore, having your loins gift about with truth, and having on the breastplate of righteousness: And your feet shod with the preparation of the gospel of peace; Above all, taking the shield of faith, wherewith ye shall be able to quench the fiery darts of the wicked. And take the helmet of salvation, and the sword of the Spirit, which is the word of God: Praying always with all prayer and supplication in the Spirit, and watching thereunto with all perseverance and supplication for all saints."

CHAPTER FIVE

The "Easy" Years

SO, IN CASE anyone out there reading is sick to death of this chick's writing about how bad life is—here you are. Here, indeed, is your "let up" for a chapter. Even here, I'm just gonna layer in and sprinkle in examples where I know God showed me so much grace and mercy.

But the "easy years"? I'm sort of chuckling, too. Your easy years are supposed to be childhood, right? Believe me when I tell you there are many of us that do not share that sentiment. Truly, for those who had an amazing childhood (not perfect, but you wish you could relive those days), I am SO happy for you! In my humble and highly biased opinion, I would rather be dragged across a bed of hot coals liberally sprinkled with big shards of glass than relive my childhood. Too honest? Well—so be it.

OK, I digress. My easier years actually started my junior and senior years in high school and went through college. My high school years, in spite of being lonely, were on the easier side academically; learning from books has never been tremendously difficult, and I am so thankful for that. It's a bit of a two-edged sword, only because my mom wouldn't stop at my doing my best—it had to be straight A's and why not A pluses? Nevertheless, that drove me to study; I enjoy studying (from books—NOT computers!!) and I am a consummate list maker, so it allowed me the satisfaction of checking boxes and scratching through to-do lists. Good stuff in my mind!

I played volleyball. I had a brief moment of angst with that my senior year—but aside from that and the multiple pairs of broken glasses, volleyball at the least helped save my sanity. I truly am grateful God allowed me to play! I ended up, all in all, playing competitive volleyball for nine years through high school and college, plus another eight years on and off playing league ball. League ball was amazing—I met some wonderful friends who I remain close to and now we can reminisce about the good ol' days! I also played softball in high school and college along with soccer, running track, tennis, in line skating…I think you get the idea. If it was a sport (aside from basketball) I played it or at least tried!

I had decent parttime jobs; my first was at a diner. Here's my first moment of grace and mercy in this period (I have no doubt there were others; I remember this one vividly and literally still bear the scars from it!!). I was putting more grease in the big fryer where we cooked French fries, onion rings, etc. The first scoopful? No issues. The second? Well OK—the utensil we used to put more solid grease in was shaped similar to a serving spoon but flatter. The third scoop? Here's the thing with metal—it heats up pretty quickly! So, the oil splashed out of the fryer and that super-hot oil landed on my arm. For those out there making the appropriate weird air sucking through your teeth noise right now, thank you and you are correct.

That hot oil landed on my hand and arm, all the way up to mid forearm close to my elbow. Immediately blisters formed. I remember screaming briefly because of the pain. The diner owner, a sweet lady (who sensed what my home life was like) came running out from the kitchen. She pulled me back to the big sinks in the kitchen and immediately put my arm under cold running water. Blisters started popping up pretty shortly thereafter. She wanted to send me to the ER; no joke, I told her no. I was so afraid of how my mom would react! She scared me more than the burn! I honestly never knew how she would respond to anything. I said no, I can keep working (man, was I stupid...). So, I took orders left handed and tried to keep my right arm out of sight!

When I finally saw the doctor about it on Monday (this happened on a Friday), he gasped. Thankfully it was a very deep second degree and not a third degree—a HUGE blessing, because I might have required skin grafts and debridements to fix it. He fussed at me for not coming in sooner. Shockingly my mom didn't yell at me when I got home that night but let me make the choice not to go to the ER—another testament of grace!! I kept working and going to school, but I still have the scars from that burn 35 years later! Oh for God's protection!!

My next job I worked as a CNA—certified nursing assistant (except when I started you didn't have to be certified...a little scary there). I was 16. After I ran away, my mom wouldn't let me work at the diner again—she partially laid blame there because, in her words, "boys kept asking me out." Sigh. Boys were a battle between us, unfortunately. More to come there. What a strange, wondrous way God works though. Lamentations 3:22–23 states "It is of the Lord's mercies that we are not consumed, because his compassions fail not. They are new every morning: great is thy faithfulness." Friends, let me tell you—I was very book smart, but so terribly naïve—and yet God showed me mercy and extended grace—seemingly by the hour!! Working at a nursing home provided such a wonderful experience for me; I had a love of taking care of people! There were some frightening moments though. I had a resident with severe dementia attack me once; praise God I was in a hallway and there were people nearby who pulled him off me!! Mostly my time there involved lots of pureed food, changing linens and occasionally chasing down naked Alzheimer's patients (that one I'll never forget!). I learned efficiency, strength, and a love for older people. I learned to treat people with dignity. I pray I always will. It cemented my decision to enter the field of medicine. Despite how I started and the mistakes I made, God showed such grace putting me there. It was also at the nursing home working the 3-11 shift I learned to like coffee, and that stands true today, I promise!!

Throughout high school and college, I worked A LOT. I mean, a lot a lot. I mean, so much. Turns out I have my dad's workaholic tendencies. Good? Bad? I think both. Idleness is not good with me. I'll find some way to occupy my time! During college, between my freshman and sophomore years, I worked 80 hours a week. I had no life that summer, but I had a goal: med school. I wanted to be a heart surgeon. One itsy bitsy problem? I have a weak muscle in my left eye that prevents me from focusing very closely. In fact, when I'm super tired or they give me muscle relaxers or certain meds before surgery, my eye will "go for a walk." It's actually pretty entertaining for others to watch but super weird when I can feel it happening. My husband has his own name for it that I won't share, per his request. It's not good for someone wielding a surgical instrument though!

I went to a very conservative Christian college in South Carolina called Bob Jones University. There are things to be said, both negative and positive, about it. Did I agree with all the rules? Nope. Did I sign a paper that I would follow the rules? Yup. Did I break some of the rules anyway? Yup. Was it a sin to do so? Yes, it was. Did God forgive me and protect me? For so many times YES. (Now, before you think I went hog wild, I did not. I was very busy studying!) There were a few occasions where I did and was never caught by administration. Did God know? Of course, He did. There was one incident where I felt I was treated very unfairly, and I was correct—but in retrospect, I honestly feel that one incident sort of balanced out some of the other times God showed mercy and didn't allow me to get caught!

So, what did I learn there? So many things. At BJU, pretty much everybody graduates with a minor in Bible. I learned to memorize verses by the hundreds. Thankfully, I have a good memory, and I still remember many of those verses. Between Awana as a child and Bible doctrines class, I firmly believe in hiding God's word in your heart. (For those not familiar with Awana, it is a kids' Bible program, and it includes ages two through the teenage years. Awana stands for Approved Workmen Are Not Ashamed.) Not only will it primarily help you not sin against God (Psalm 119:11, paraphrased by me), but those verses the Holy Spirit will bring to your remembrance. He has done so over and over again for me! John 14:26 states, "But the Comforter, which is the Holy Ghost, whom the Father will send in my name, he shall teach you all things, and bring all things to your remembrance, whatsoever I have said unto you." I am so thankful for the promises of Jesus there!

Other good things? Time management. Study habits. A social life!!! Thankfully I was always self-motivated; I actually enjoyed studying. I am a firm believer that if you put forth your best effort, truly, that God will honor that. We are commanded as Christians "Whether therefore ye eat, or drink, or whatsoever ye do, do all to the glory of God" (I Corinthians 10:31). As I moved along in my studies, I learned to pray over those tests I took and papers I wrote—they got much harder! My freshman and sophomore years were not as challenging, but I had heavy course loads. Moving into those upper science courses brought me to my knees more than once!

Now, was it all studying? Nope!! In spite of the fact that there were a tremendous number of rules, I was able to have so much freedom in one regard: I had friends!! Honestly, I've really always loved being around people. Yes, there were and have been times I needed quiet, but I love laughing and having fun! I was able to pick my own friends; in a strange way it was "safe" there. Do bad things happen on Christian campuses? Yes. That wasn't my experience, thankfully—after putting myself in some stupid situations both before and after college, my personal experience was one of safety. I was able to make more choices for myself, and I learned to deal with the consequences. My mom had a favorite phrase— you make your bed, you lay in it. I still use that phrase. It always made me reflect on the consequences of my actions and it caused me to stop and think before I did a lot of stupid things, saving me from some disasters!! I am thankful for that phrase!

I was truly blessed at Bob Jones to meet some wonderful friends, many of whom I still talk to today. The one person I met at Bob Jones that has been an amazing example of a Biblical friend is my best friend, Wendy. She truly is the Jonathan to my David; the friends that sticks closer than a brother; the "iron that sharpeneth iron" friend that I am far and away so humbly thankful for. We have been "besties" for 31 years and counting. There were a couple of years where we were not in touch as much, which I regret; time and circumstances can do that on occasion. There is just not enough I can say to thank God for this amazing woman God has placed in my life. We have wept together, howled laughing together, prayed together, sang together...we have seen pretty much every facet of each other there is to see. And still, she seems to like me!!! We have "shared" each other's kids—she is Aunt Wendy to mine, and I was either Aunt Mel or Mrs. Mel to hers—now hers are adults and they are "allowed" to call me Melanie.

It's difficult to put into words how much grace this woman has extended to me; the grace that God bestowed upon me sending me this sister of my soul!! I cannot thank Him enough! She has provided strength to lean on, wise counsel, a listening ear, a shoulder to cry on—there is nothing I cannot or would not tell her, and her to me; I'm sure there have been moments she has wished I wasn't so transparent with her but here we are!! There will be some "Wendy moments" sprinkled through here...

Another person I meet while I was in college is my now and still ever enduring (bless his heart!!) husband, Frank. He is a man of many nicknames—Frankito, Hoob (thusly named because he tried to call me "wifey" and he spelled it "wiffy"—I was just returning the favor...), the Frankster...you get the idea. Yes, he features pretty prominently since, again, bless his heart...he has stuck by my side for 26 years of marriage and a couple of years on and off dating. So without further adieu, let me introduce you to this saint…

Franky and I met working at the pizza place behind Bob Jones. I started working there my sophomore year and worked there through my senior year and even after that. Honestly, I loved it there. I seriously love cooking!! I had worked at Burger King up in Pennsylvania between years at college and loved that, too! The other upside to working at a pizza place is free pizza!! I had some awesome coworkers there so even on the really busy nights it was still a blast. It was also way more chill than studying biochemistry, physics, organic chemistry, and histology—to name a few. It served as a place to escape when we had Artist Series, which were attempts to give us sheltered college students some culture and for the girls to show off fancy dresses, hair, and makeup. I didn't mind the Shakespeare plays; I actually enjoyed them. But the operas? Holy Moses. Let's just say I made sure I scheduled myself to work those nights—one of my other good college friends and I went together to an opera with subtitles, and we proceeded to spend four hours making up our own storyline. We pretty much laughed our makeup off and got glared at a good bit. I didn't date very much at Bob Jones—between my heavy course load and work schedule there wasn't time. Add to that my "super-sized" personality—folks, I'm just a lot. Let's just say I'm thankful I wasn't called to be a preacher's wife but to work with surgeons—again, God's grace in extending the right calling to each of us!! I have (mostly) made peace with my personality, because I haven't figured out how to scale back yet!

Anyhoo, my poor beleaguered now hubby had already been work-ing at Little Caesar's for a couple of years when I started there. He's just over a year older than me, and at the time he was taking college courses as well. He is an artist and is very smart in his own way, but he is quiet where I am LOUD. He is polite and reserved and I'm…not. He is shy and I can talk to light fixtures and have a perfectly good conversation. So, let's say when he asked me out the first time…well, I thought he was joking, and I told him that. Oops. He was serious…I can't lie, ours was not the classic "butterflies" or love at first sight kind of love story. I didn't melt when I saw him. He just quietly wormed his way into my heart. Nothing wrong with love at first sight!! It just wasn't our experience!! We finally did start dating my second semester my senior year when I moved off campus.

In truth, I dated very little before him. I had one boyfriend prior to dating him. I used to be a shameless, terrible flirt. May I warn the young ladies out there reading this? Don't. Do. That. Do not!! Your reputation can end up tattered—thank you Jesus for Your grace and protection there!! You can also end up in some very tenuous situations. In NO WAY am I placing blame on girls for being attacked, hurt, raped—in NO WAY, and there is no excuse for it…just, guard yourselves. Be careful. There are ways to have fun without getting yourself in a precarious situation. Also, do not try to find love in the physical alone. That country song looking for love in all the wrong places? It's so easy to fall prey to an attraction seeming like love. Pray before you get into a relationship. Seek what Jesus would want for you, which is your husband to love you as Christ loves the church. Heal your hearts—this is a big one, folks. Let Jesus heal you where you have been hurt before you jump into a relationship. A loving spouse should lead you to a stronger Christian life; he should support, lead, and encourage you in your walk with God. However—we are all human beings, and we WILL fail each other. It's so important to learn to extend grace to each other! OK, dating advice done. Back to the story.

Now, I will say…want to talk about grace here? How about married 26 plus years…a family background like mine. Financial issues (major at times). A special needs child. My mom becoming addicted to narcotics, a failed suicide attempt, a stroke, and succumbing to death by house fire. Four years later, my sister committed suicide. One of my best friends had brain surgery then died at work a year and a half later. My father-in-law died. My brother-in-law shot himself in the head and died. My dad had a major stroke and died. Did I mention our autistic child? In there as well, my husband had heart surgery, and I've since had eleven surgeries. We have had two miscarriages. Moved a couple of times. That, folks…26 years of marriage. Threats of divorce. Some close calls with terrible decisions on my part. I've worked third shift for the past almost 25 years and at times 60 hours a week. And yet, despite all that, here we are. That. Is. Grace. Is life perfect? Clearly and obviously not. I have no doubt there are days he would love to push me off the side of a mountain. I would return that favor some days. After surviving what we have together, we still manage to laugh like rabid monkeys until are crying—and we have managed in the harshness of life to stay together. We are not ones to fight with each other. I grew up in a harsh, contentious, hostile house and I just cannot abide it; I do tend to "bury" things and just flat ignore others I know I can't change to keep the peace. The best way? Not necessarily. But what we have learned after all these years is there are some things that won't change. My daughter has pretty severe autism and an alphabet soup of other diagnoses; she is who she is.

We have talked about what we could have done differently. Sometimes you've just got to stop beating the horse that is well and truly dead. Can you change the past? Nope. Can you learn from past mistakes and not repeat them? Absolutely. Yes…there have been times when after the kids have gone to bed, we have gone "radio silent" on each other; he will paint or read, I will crochet or waste time playing Farmville or something useless. During the day I'll likely put in some good gospel music and sing the house down while I'm baking or cooking before work.

So where do I see grace throughout our marriage? The early years of our marriage truly were easy years. There were those few years where God just seemed to look down and say, enjoy this…have some time just together…we hiked, we got away, we would go for long walks in the dark together. I miss those days! I can't lie. But even that, in my little mind, is evidence of grace to be able to look back and see the gift of those moments together when life was carefree. We have experienced some tremendous answers to prayer—what grace there!!! The fact that God even listens to my prayers is grace—I sure don't deserve for Him to hear me, but praise Jesus that through His righteousness I can come to the throne of grace! There have been times we, like Paul, prayed for healing or changing and God allowed it not to happen—just like everyone has had! We have had bills paid that we didn't have money for; found "just the right" van that we could afford. So many moments of our marriage showed mercy and grace.

Where else do I see grace in those "easy years" of high school and college? First, even though I only had one option for college according to my mom, it was the right option for me. Another example of God using some craptastic decisions on my part to lead me to the place He wanted me to be. Second, during this time I also met my other best friend Kristen—she was pivotal in not only being at my church now, but also being in my career and current job as a nurse. God blessed me greatly, again, giving me another soul sister as a friend! Our bond is deep—there are times we don't see each other except at church for a few weeks at a time, but we are always there to support each other, and we have each other's backs. So much grace and so many incredible memories we have together. Third, during this time we finally found our home church—and 20 years later we are still there. I can't even begin to tell you those stories of grace and mercy, how our lives have changed being there; our church has been a shelter for me, a place where I could let myself relax in Jesus and feel His presence with my fellow believers. It's a place where I feel more at home than I think anywhere else than, well, home.

How do I sum up my church? Now, don't get me wrong...we are far from perfect there. I'm not stupid—if I'm feeling like I'm fighting Satan with a water pistol some days I'm sure every other person feels that way. But oh the GRACE I have experienced there. I have been so blessed to be able to sing in the choir the past 19 years. The untold moments of just the right sermon preached that I needed, the song my soul thirsted for, that friend coming up and saying just what you needed to hear, times praying at the altar where someone joined you or you were able to come and pray with someone else. I'm so humbled to be there and experience those precious moments God has given me. We started going there in our "easy years," but our church family has sustained us through some very dark and stormy years. I have friendships with singers that come every year for our revival services; these precious folks are dear friends that I wouldn't have gotten to meet had I not been at Temple. So many "right place at the right time" moments God has given us there. So many opportunities to serve Him! So many wonderful people I have had the privilege to meet that have prayed for me, with me, and been an example for me. God makes no mistakes—our way might seem a little convoluted, but His path has a purpose. I can see now so many times a sermon, a person, a song would not only affect me at the time, but I would be able to reflect on for years to come. I am so very blessed!

Point of reflection: When you think back on some "easy years" or "good years", did you feel closer or farther from God? Did you tend to rest on your own strength or accomplishments? Were you thankful for the periods of time out of the deeper valleys? On occasion I'm guilty when times are "easier" of forgetting to praise God—to thank God—to still rely on Him. I occasionally fall prey to thinking I earned something by my hard work; in reality all we have comes from God.

Psalm 16:7–8, 11 states "I will bless the Lord, who hath given me counsel: my reins also instruct me in the night seasons. 8 I have set the Lord always before me: because he is at my right hand, I shall not be moved. 11 Thou wilt shew me the path of life: in thy presence is fulness of joy: at thy right hand there are pleasures for evermore."

CHAPTER SIX

My Defiant Years

LET'S FACE IT, folks—I doubt there are many of us out there who couldn't look back through an entire section, big or small, of our lives and not facepalm ourselves. Here's what amazes me—that even when we, as Christians, are deliberately "sowing our wild oats," in our rumspringa, to borrow an Amish term—God can and will show us grace and mercy. I look back on this period and think, oh God—literally, oh God—I sure did not deserve for You to "seemingly" overlook these blatant sins! (That doesn't happen, by the way—He sees all! He was just waiting for me to come back to myself!). I'm astoundingly, amazingly grateful that God did not dole out what I could have reaped—that He continued to show me mercy upon mercy and grace upon grace!

I'm going to keep this chapter brief—seriously. Not because I won't own up to my buckets of mistakes, but because my focus of this book is on God's grace! Here is the short story: my heart was chock full of bitterness and hurt. People, bitterness and hurt will eat you alive. I watched my mom deal with bitterness all her life with her family upbringing. You would have thought seeing that I could have prevented or stepped away from the negative thought cycle. Nope! I battled for a long time with terrible bitterness. Do I still have times when I battle it? Yup. Praise God, not like I did. We all deal with bitterness and buried pain. I had a terrible time for the longest time accepting God's limitless love. I still have moments. Relationships still prove difficult. I learned early on in life that allowing people to get close to you means you are vulnerable—and boy howdy can people hurt you! I held pretty much everybody at arm's length, and I trusted very few people not to hurt me. When someone got close, I backed off!!

Add to that, so many years being raised in a Christian school (a blessing, right?) and a Christian university—the very places I should have been learning and cultivating the good things of God! But my battered and distrustful heart could only see what I was missing. Folks—I was missing love. Again, I was saved. We pray in my prayer group at church now every week for prodigals—I pray I never end up in that place ever again!! Oh, though, what God has taught me…and as brief as that period was, I'm so thankful that what looked at the time like "common sense" was the Holy Ghost just prompting me home….

For all the bad I grew up with, one thing I wasn't raised with was alcohol. My paternal grandfather was a mean, abusive alcoholic—I've already referred to him earlier. So, my dad was not big at all on drinking. He would, on occasion after a hot summer day's work, have a beer. Funny story, though—I have to include this. He went to a company picnic on Saturday in the summer (I don't remember how old I was, but I was very young)—he loved pitching horseshoes, and he was good at it. They had an impromptu horseshoe pitching tournament, which he won. His coworkers decided to celebrate his win by plying him with alcohol—and they mixed beer and liquor, which I'm told it's a big no no. At this time, my mom had taken my brother and I to her best friend's house to swim in their pool. We got home late—I'm assuming after 9pm because it was dark—and came home to see vomit up the stairs. Just… random puddles of it.

Now—here's the kicker—we lived in half a duplex, and there was precisely one, count 'em, one—bathroom. No other toilets or showers. We went up the stairs and there is my dad passed out cold in front of the toilet. Folks, the man was 6'3" and about 240 lbs. He was a bear of a man. And there was no budging his unconscious self. To add to it, he had vomited his dentures into the toilet. We clearly had a dilemma—my brother and I had to get ready for bed and everybody had to pee. What to do? I looked over at my mom and said, what do we do? Mom being mom—she pulled no punches. Compassion was not her strong suit. Her reply? Use the toilet like normal. Wait, whaaaa??? I asked her if she was going to fish his dentures out. Nope! To compound things even more, my dad was such a big guy that he literally took up all the space from the toilet to the door. So, we did what we had to—we used the toilet then stood on his back to brush our teeth. The next day, by the time we got up, the stairs were cleaned, the bathroom was clean, and the toilet was clean and dentureless. After that my dad didn't touch alcohol for 20 years!!

That being said, after I graduated from Bob Jones and moved away from Pennsylvania back to South Carolina (I lived at home from May 1994 to January 1995), I admit—I had some moments. Being raised in a household where rules were strict, but no alternatives given…no explanation—just do as I'm told—or even different don't do something because you'll be like your sister—moving and being by myself turned into "no one can tell me what to do anymore." When I share these thoughts, in no way am I trying to justify my actions, merely explain the thought processes behind them.

Romans 6:1–2 says "What shall we say then? Shall we continue in sin, that grace may abound? God forbid. How shall we, that are dead to sin, live any longer therein?" In no way am I trying to justify my actions. I will say, though, that I am once again thankful that I haven't had to live with effects from some of those decisions. God surely showed me mercy! I wanted to touch on one thing quickly as well…my choice of the word defiant. I was outwardly defiant during this time, but that defiance starts with a wrong heart attitude. My defiance stemmed from feeling like I had to always do what was told or I would be "bad" or compared to someone else...I outwardly obeyed but inwardly I rebelled. That was more my defiance than anything. Until you fix a heart problem, you can be outwardly obedient and still struggle with sin in your heart.

Alcohol is a heated topic in the Christian world. This is my book, and this is my rationale. I am a teetotaler. I tried alcohol during that period after college and it did NOT agree with me. First thing I tried was something with vodka—being Russian that should work out fine, right? WRONG. I remember calling my husband sobbing—I had had maybe a fourth of a mixed drink with vodka while I was out with some friends—we will talk about the influence of friends in a minute—and just decided it was what I would do. Anyone else find out that alcohol was a depressant the hard way? Just me?

My other few attempts at alcohol (and it was literally maybe four other times) didn't end well, either. A sniff makes me woozy, and a quarter of a drink and I'm done. Praise God for His favor! It's weird to realize that even there, God's grace was extended and protected me! I think of Psalm 139:14a where David states "I am fearfully and wonderfully made." This is definitely a time where I'm thankful God made my weird system as He did!!

So, the friend thing...I've always wanted friends. Lots of friends. Struggled hard with being such a lonely little kid in school...high school, I wasn't really "allowed" to have friends. My mom really trusted no one by that point in time unless she was there—even with church functions. College? OOOH!! I could pick my own friends!! Now at Bob Jones, not such a big deal—there were all these rules, you see, so it was difficult to get in trouble there. But after college, in that defiant time of my life, I chose to become friends with people who did not encourage me in my walk with Jesus. Was I still a Christian? Yes. Did they know that? Yes. I got made fun of a little, but thankfully not much—although I wonder if they had pushed more, I might not have leaned away from them and back towards Jesus. To my young ladies out there—surround yourself with friends who love Jesus, too! Who you hang around with definitely impacts your decisions, especially when you're young and very impressionable!! Those same friends who claim they will always be there for you might very well be the same people who walk away when you get in trouble!

Here's my biggest confession, and some of you may laugh—I am. A. Flirt. Oh my word. The hot water I've nearly landed myself in and the shame I've dealt with—oh my WORD. By nature, I'm talkative and friendly. I love hugs. BIG hugs. Love them!! Combine the feeling of not being good enough, being a flirt, feeling like you're already worthless, and unfortunately not having the best judgment with boys/men when I was younger, and it could have spelled a powder keg of disaster. BUT GOD. Truthfully, He sure could have let me pay the consequences of my actions. There were times He did, sure. But not nearly to the degree that He rightfully should have—and that, friends, is MERCY. Whew!!

As much of a flirt as I was, truthfully getting close to men scared me a little. Honestly, I struggled to believe them when they paid me compliments or flattered me. I sure did try for a little bit to make myself feel loved. Two big moments of grace here: the biggest by far was a heavenly Father who would, by the prompting of the Holy Spirit, put almost a "hard stop" on when things got pushed too far. I am eternally grateful—again—that God thumped me hard enough on the head that I listened to His still small voice!

Now, before anyone out there starts doing math or gets this terrible opinion of me that I made a list of rounds—I didn't. Things didn't get "that far" but one time; even then, when your mind, heart, and body are all that involved…it's too far! There is so much to be said to coming into your marriage with your virtue and innocence intact and something precious to share with only your spouse, and I wish I could say that was my experience but sadly it wasn't. Ladies—listen and listen well.

IT IS NOT WORTH IT. Your value in Jesus, your self-worth, your conscience, your choices, your entire life can be affected by those poor choices (it's sin, folks—let me just call it what it is). If I can caution any young lady, preserve your modesty. The attention you may get from overly revealing clothing? Not worth it. (Please trust me and don't think I'm being judgmental!!) The short-term gratification you may get from being wrapped up with the wrong man? NOT WORTH IT!

The other example of grace during this time—I had watched my older sister make so many bad choices with men. I will not degrade her—I'll leave it there—but I saw the consequences of her choices and her decisions lived out in front of me. She had to live with those consequences and there were times the price was very high. In so many ways I had an epic battle with my sister over her actions in life—a part of me was angry because everything I did was compared to her, a large part of me felt pity for her. I had so much fear of her as well—she had an awful temper, and she was really abusive at times. Yet still, I see shadows of God's grace here because He allowed me to see how her actions affected her and others. I also learned to be truthful and be kind based on her actions. She is proof, to me, that what some may use for evil God could use for good.

I debated—hard—about whether or not to put this little section in this chapter. The deciding factor? Listening to a friend of mine talk about tattoos and piercings. No, I don't have tattoos. Honestly? I can't stand them. It's not for Biblical reasons—it's a knee jerk reaction. You see, the same sister that I got compared to was covered in tattoos; the reaction stems from that…I equate tattoos with her. Piercings as well. Before the question pops into your mind, no, I don't care if you have your ears pierced—I've had mine pierced three times and all three times they had to be removed (turns out I'm extremely sensitive to metals—I know, be amazed!). And for the sake of shock, I did get my navel pierced—not once but twice. The first time was directly related to "I'm sick of being compared to her." Anyone else have a moment like that or just me? I didn't get that piercing because I was so terribly enamored of it—it was my little secret. I didn't wear clothing where it could be seen easily; so why did I do it? Flat. Out. Defiance. It was absolutely my heart being not attuned to my Savior. The second time? Let's just label it some bizarre form of midlife crisis and leave it right there. Am I absolutely against tattoos and piercings as a whole? For me, I just don't like how they look. They're just not my thing, and they represent a time of rebellion where my heart and actions were not lined up with God at all. That's probably my biggest personal issue with them.

I said all that to say this—I struggle with being judgmental about that issue because I personally do not like them. I lost a good friend because I opened my mouth and voiced an opinion and grace was nowhere to be found in that opinion. I did apologize but the damage was done. My thoughts? Err on the side of grace. Maybe that person you're judging for having some (to you) awful looking tattoo has never been shown the love of God. Maybe they just got saved. Maybe they've been saved for a long time and those tattoos are part of their testimony now. I wish I had learned a long time ago that my holier than thou opinion won't do much at all to point people to my Savior.

Point of reflection: We have all, at some point, had periods of defiance—some of us moments, some of us days, months, or years. What brought you "back to your senses"? Luke 15 tells the story of the prodigal son. Verse 17 said the son "came to himself." What prompted you, in your situation, to turn back to God and repent? What happened to cause you to consistently follow His leading again? I'm not talking about a sin you deal with right away like a moment of anger, frustration, etc. God's very goodness leads us back to Him!

I John 1:9—"If we confess our sins, he is faithful and just to forgive us our sins, and to cleanse us from all unrighteousness."

Romans 2:4—"Or despisest thou the riches of his goodness and forbearance and longsuffering; not knowing that the goodness of God leadeth to repentance?"

CHAPTER SEVEN

What Does the Bible say about Grace?

AFTER EVERYTHING I'VE written I felt this was a good place to insert more of the authority of the holy Word of God. By no means did I do a full, comprehensive, write-down-every-verse-associated-with-grace Bible search. I did write down a tremendous number of verses, and I don't feel like I even scratched the surface of what the Bible says about grace.

First of all, where do we see grace first mentioned in the Bible? Genesis 6:8 says, "But Noah found grace in the eyes of the Lord." In the midst of a time riddled with sin and seemingly bereft of God's presence, there was a man who encountered His grace. Unless I counted wrong (and that's entirely possible!) I counted 38 references with the word grace in them in the Old Testament; but in the New Testament there were 122 references to grace! This didn't totally surprise me, knowing that the Old Testament is widely referred to as the time of the law and the New Testament as the time of grace. In the New Testament we have Jesus;

born of a virgin, died on a cross, and rose again!! This allowed, with a person's believing in Jesus and accepting His free gift of salvation (grace!) and the end of the eternal separation between God and man!!

Grace was still applied and seen in use in the Old Testament! There aren't many references to grace in the books of the law. Moses was initially given the Ten Commandments by God on Mt. Sinai and more specifics of the law that the Jews adhered to. But grace was still present!! God did allow communication between Himself and man; the sacrifices the Israelites made (the shedding of animal blood in most cases) with an attitude of humbling and contriteness allowed acceptance of those sacrifices. Those sacrifices were never ending during that time because the blood of animals was temporary—the blood of Jesus in the New Testament is the only permanent acceptable sacrifice for our sins!! Some of the Old Testament examples of grace we see were in Ruth, Esther, and Psalms. These three books contained the most references to grace and centered on the lives of Ruth, Esther, and David.

In the story of Ruth, we see the title character who stayed and supported her mother-in-law, Naomi, who had lost her husband and both sons. Ruth and her sister-in-law Orpah were both Moabites, traditionally enemies of Israel. Ruth is well known for her devotion to Naomi, and our modern-day wedding vows have some basis in Ruth 1:16-17 where she vows she will stay with Naomi. Where do I see grace come in? The unmerited favor in this story is seen when Ruth went and gleaned (picked up the leftovers) from Boaz's fields. Ruth 2:2 finds Ruth telling Naomi she will "glean ears of corn after him in whose sight I shall find grace." God had perfect knowledge of whose fields she was going to, and how He could indeed work all things to Ruth's and Naomi's good. Ruth 2:10 has Ruth asking Boaz "why have I found grace in thine eyes, that thou shouldest take knowledge of me, seeing I am a stranger?" His answer? Boaz had been told how Ruth was loyal to Naomi, and he in turn had developed great respect for Ruth. It seems like her grace was "earned" by her loyalty, but it was truly a gift that she couldn't pay the price for!

Esther tells the story of a beautiful young Jewish woman who is chosen to be the bride of a powerful foreign king. Esther 2:17a states, "And the king loved Esther above all women, and she obtained grace and favor in his sight more than all the virgins; so that he set the royal crown upon her head." Why did Esther obtain grace? The only thing that seemed to set her apart was found in Esther 2:7 and 2:15; she was "fair and beautiful" and "required nothing but what Hegai the king's chamberlain, the keeper of the women, appointed." Doesn't seem terribly important, does it? And possibly we are left somewhat in the dark—but clearly Esther had been given unmerited favour! Without a doubt God had allowed Esther to be given this grace! She boldly used this favor to help save the lives of many Israelites later in the book.

In the book of Psalms, written mostly by David, we see in his life example after example of grace and mercy. David was chosen by God and despite many painful failures he confessed his sins and retained God's favour. Grace, in both Psalms and Proverbs, are promised to those who walk uprightly and keep God's commandments. Psalms 84:11 states, "For the LORD God is a sun and shield: the LORD will give grace and glory: no good thing will he withhold from them that walk uprightly." Proverbs 1:8-9 state, "My son, hear the instruction of thy father, and forsake not the law of thy mother: For they shall be an ornament of grace unto thy head, and chains about thy neck." In Proverbs, wisdom and grace go hand in hand. Proverbs 4:9 states, "She (wisdom) shall give to thine head an ornament of grace: a crown of glory shall she deliver to thee."

What of the New Testament? The most references to grace in any book in the Bible are found in Romans, with 20 references to grace in this book alone. Grace is a powerful central theme of Romans. First, grace is from God (Romans 1:5,7). God's grace justifies us—Romans 3:24 states "Being justified freely by his grace through the redemption that is in Christ Jesus." Romans chapters 4 and 5 show us that grace is given by God and the way we can have this free gift is by our faith—not our works!! We are utterly, thoroughly dependent on God for our salvation—it is an exercise of our faith that yields this grace and not something any person can "earn." That being stated, in Romans 6 we are encouraged as believers to live righteous, holy lives; not using God's free gift of grace as an excuse or license to sin. Romans 6:14-15: "For sin shall not have dominion over you: for ye are not under the law, but under grace. What then? Shall we sin, because we are not under the law, but under grace? God forbid." Romans 12:3,6 tells us that we are given different gifts through God's grace. Why is that? The answer is in I Corinthians 12 where we learn about the body of Christ being one body with many members.

Allow me, for a moment, to "step outside the sermon" as my pastor would say. And no, I am NOT preaching!! (Just borrowing a phrase. He uses lots of good phrases!) Can I, once again, tell you how much I love music? (Go ahead—roll your eyes out loud. I do it plenty, so join me!) I love gospel music. I love the harmony, the messages—you get the point. What would I love to do? Be a singer! Yup, you read it here. Oh, I would love it. I am my own concert in my car—you can ask my girls! I have made many loaves of bread, cakes, cheesecakes, etc. harmonizing to something—I have my favorites! (I think they taste better when sung to, but that could just be me!) Anyhoo, what's my point? For goodness' sake, why don't I just grab a mic and go for it?

STAGE FRIGHT. Yup. The whole "center of attention" thing. Do I have an ok voice? Yeah, I do. "Choir voice." (Don't worry, I just made that up.) Well, what do I do for a living? I'm a critical care nurse. I take care of open-heart surgery patients. What part of the body am I in the body of Christ? Well, as a nurse, I sure use my hands a lot. So. Much. Am I the hands of Jesus? I sure hope and pray so. Maybe the feet of Jesus as well, walking up and down halls. Would I love to be the mouth? To sing for Him? Well, yeah…I would. But what has God equipped me for? In His holy, omniscient, ever-present grace, did He equip me to be what He called me to be? YES. A thousand million times yes. Do I always use that to His glory? I fail. I do. I get irritated at work—whine and complain—yup. But am I equipped for what He has called for? Yes. Can

I still have a love for music? Absolutely! Does music touch me, stir my soul so my calling is easier? Yes! The body works together—or it should!! I am so incredibly thankful for Christian artists who God has equipped to do their calling as either writers or singers (or both) who make my calling easier!

That calling? What we are in the body of Christ? It comes from grace. I Corinthians 15:10 states "But by the grace of God I am what I am: and his grace which was bestowed upon me was not in vain." The strength to continue on in our lives is also from grace. II Corinthians 12:9a—"And he said unto me, My grace is sufficient for thee: for my strength is made perfect in weakness. Most gladly therefore will I rather glory in my infirmities, that the power of Christ may rest upon me." Ephesians 4:7—"But unto every one of us is given grace according to the measure of the gift of Christ." We have grace every day. Some days I know I need more—how do we get more from the eternal source? Hebrews 4:16 gives us the answer—"Let us therefore come boldly unto the throne of grace, that we may obtain mercy, and find grace to help in time of need." All we need to do is ask! God will grant the mercy and grace that we need! James 4:6a says, "But he giveth more grace." II Peter 3:18 states, "But grow in grace, and in the knowledge of our Lord and Savior Jesus Christ. To Him be glory both now and forever. Amen."

How can I emphasize enough the amazing miracle of grace? I truly feel like I can go on and on for days just pulling in more Scripture. I will try to summarize.

Grace is free. Grace is a gift.

Grace outlines our spiritual gifts and our "job" in the body of Christ—and allows us to fulfill that work!

Grace comes from God's never-ending supply!

Grace and faith work together—when we pray in faith asking for additional grace, it is supplied!

Grace is not an excuse or license to sin—the exact opposite—it should cause us to refrain from sin.

Grace should cause us to grow as Christians—we should mature with it!

The same grace God extends to us, we in turn need to exercise with others and extend to them.

GRACE WILL CHANGE YOU.

CHAPTER EIGHT

Has Grace Changed Me?

"How Saved I Am"

—Triumphant Quartet,
Bigger than Sunday CD, 2021. (6)

I still remember who I used to be,
When this heart cried out to be free,
I was desperate, a failure, in need of a Savior.
And I still remember the moment, the time
When I finally surrendered my life
I was broken and ran into arms wide open!

Oh what a difference He made in me!
Because of the blood I'm forgiven and free!
Everything changed the moment His mercy found me, found me
Now every sin has been traded for grace,
Love came and washed away every stain

I'll testify over and over again, how lost I was, how saved I am!
Maybe you're thinking you're too far gone,
You can't get to the cross from the road that you're on.
But He'll find you—right there—trust me, I've been there!

Oh what a difference He made in me!
Because of the blood I'm forgiven and free!
Everything changed the moment His mercy found me, found me
Every sin has been traded for grace,
Love came and washed away every stain
I'll testify over and over again—how lost I was, how saved I am!

I'm praising my Savior all the day long,
This is my story, this is my song!

Oh what a difference He made in me,
Because of the blood I'm forgiven and free!
Everything changed the moment His mercy found me, found me
Now every sin has been traded for grace,
Love came and washed away every stain!
I'll testify over and over again—over and over again,
How lost I was, how saved I am!

This is my story, this is my song
Praising my Savior all the day long!

FOR THOSE WHO haven't heard this song, reading the words may
not touch your heart like it does mine. If you don't love music like I do,
maybe it won't. But oh, the enormity of this song for me—when I reflect
on the change that grace has made in my life. WOW is just inadequate.
When you are listening to this at midnight with tears streaming down
your face, hands raised in praise—yes, what a difference grace has made!

I just saw something on Facebook (and OF COURSE I can't find it again!)…I'm going to try to rephrase this…because this morning, as soon as my eyes opened Satan started. You can't write this book on grace. You're struggling with these thoughts; your faith is weak…YOU? Write a book on grace? Well, good morning to you too Satan (please note: never once have I wished the devil good morning, but I sure wish he would wait until I had some coffee and Bible reading in me before he started in on me). What inspiring thing did I see, you may ask? A powerful reminder. No, I am NOT worthy, on my own, to write a book about God's grace. I am not worthy, on my own, to do anything for His kingdom. But what's more important? I am not doing this ON MY OWN. By the righteousness of Jesus, I can write this book, and only through that! Because I accepted His free gift of salvation, because the blood of Jesus has paid my sin debt, because of GRACE I can write about grace! So Satan—your words don't matter. As another friend posted, don't let Satan keep you prisoner to your past! My future in Jesus is secure! Even though, without a doubt, I will fail Jesus today and every day, as much as I yearn not to, He will still lovingly forgive me, and His righteousness gives me the ability to come back to God!

Well hallelujah—who needs dark roast coffee now? (I'm going to drink some anyway…) Friends, yes—I have been changed by grace. Have I let Satan defeat me before, even knowing I am a blood bought, redeemed, child of the most High God? Yes. Will he possibly cause me defeat in the future, at least temporarily? Unfortunately, yes. Will he dance around with glee when I fail God and sin? Yup—it's what he does. But his delight is short lived, and his defeat is sure! Delight not in what you have in you—delight yourself in the Lord and who you are in God! Remember what He has given you and what He has redeemed you from!! Straighten your crown—you are a child of the King!

So the answer is so much yes, grace has changed me. You've seen some of my story by now and how God worked those golden threads through what sure felt like some ugly dark tapestry and managed to bring beauty from ashes. How God can turn broken into beautiful. If I ever work up the nerve to sing a song, it will be Broken into Beautiful—Karen Peck sings it. If there was a song I could claim as mine, this is it. The beautiful part isn't referring to physical beauty, but spiritual beauty. It's a song about a broken, shattered past that only God can redeem and turn into something glorious for Him. I pray that He will keep using me for Him. Look that song up—it's amazing.

Grace has allowed me to forgive what seems unforgivable.

Grace has made my unlovable self feel and know love.

Grace has broken chains and set my soul free.

Grace has taken a hard, bitter heart and made it soft and tender in the hands of the Master.

Grace has taken a broken girl and turned her into a whole person.

Do I still have healing to do? YES! Is there work to be done still? YES. Am I complete? Nope. I'm not in heaven yet, so I'm still a work in progress—my race is not fully run. Am I so much different than what I was and who I was? A resounding yes.

If I haven't bored you to tears yet, keep reading more of my story and see more of where God's amazing grace continues to work.

Point of reflection: How has grace changed you? Can you identify times, places, or people and know that God in His grace has moved in your life like a cool breeze on a hot day?

My challenge: try to find something every day that you can reflect on where you have experienced the grace of God in that very day. I promise—it will change your attitude and your heart. It will renew your mind and refresh your spirit.

Hebrews 4:16—"Let us therefore come boldly unto the throne of grace, that we may obtain mercy, and find grace to help in time of need." II Chronicles 16:8 says, "Give thanks unto the Lord, call upon his name, make known his deeds among the people." Verses 34 states, "O give thanks unto the Lord, for he is good; for his mercy endureth forever." I assure you, I'm guilty of overlooking where God's grace has made a difference in my daily life. So many times, we come to God's throne of grace to beg for grace but forget to thank Him when He grants us what we ask!!

CHAPTER NINE

Faith, Family, and Fortitude

HERE BEGINS THE story of how I became a nurse and when we started our family—because you should always have at least two or maybe three major life changes going on at one time!! (I'm kidding, folks!) Yay! So much goodness, right? Well, my friend, read on. There is much grace here, but some battles as well. My limited, small-vision experience? You don't necessarily see boundless, limitless grace in good times, at least not in my experience. Is grace there in those small moments? Absolutely! I can tell in my own experience that I also tend to be far more forgetful of God when life is good, and I tend to take Him more for granted. May God always remind me of His goodness!

I started working at the hospital I'm at now in 1997. I was working in the lab—now here's a moment of grace. When I went to interview for that job, I was dressed in shorts and a T shirt. No joke. I had no confidence in myself at that point; I had been fired without reason from another job I had enjoyed and was back working at a pizza place. Times were hard for my new hubby and me. We ate pizza or bread sticks every day; we budgeted and scrimped. No movies, no dinner dates. We took walks. We went hiking. In some ways, for us, it was a sweet time. I had put on a fair amount of weight and all the exercise and not eating out helped—a big moment of grace! Plus, our food budget was small—only around $40 every two weeks—so no extras! I look back and see how God was protecting us then—how He was helping protect my health and my marriage and I am grateful. At times, though, with money being so tight and being fired four months previously along with not at all using my degree, I felt ashamed.

So, I went and interviewed with the manager at the time in the lab. Not professionally dressed and discouraged from a job loss. Her comment? I was overqualified! Wait, WHAT? I remember laughing and reminding her I worked at a pizza place. But my first degree is a BS in Pre-med so I had tons of science classes. Turns out to be a phlebotomist you don't need histology or vertebrate zoology! Woo hoo! In the end, I was hired. And man, can I just tell you—again—what someone may mean for evil, God surely can use that for good. That job at the blood connection? God knew that it was a dead end for me; that with the schedule I never would have gone back to school for nursing; that I never would have been exposed to the many amazing nurses that I can thank for the path I am on now. God knew I never would have met Kristen and been absorbed, fascinated, by heart surgery patients! Friends, as hard as it is, when you find yourself in what feels like terrible circumstances that you know in your heart that you have not caused—go reread the story of Joseph in Genesis. He is proof positive of God working out your life and story for you—for your good and His glory! Walk forward in faith!

While I worked drawing blood, I got to see many, many things— frequently seeing traumas, fresh open heart surgery patients, GI bleeds, etc—and I watched nurses work hard to save lives. I got to meet so many nurses and doctors, some of whom I still have the privilege of working with and learning from. But my heart? And my brain? Drawn, inexorably, to heart surgery patients. When I wasn't working, I would go hang out in CVICU (cardiovascular intensive care unit). I would watch. And listen. And my brain just yearned for this. Next thing I knew, I was hanging out with my other best friend, Kristen. Praise God, she began teaching me. Then pushing me—Mel, go back to school. This is your unit. And she was right. (She usually is—shoutout to the wise one! Ha!) But this was such grace, that God would direct, lead, and guide me to that hospital, at that time, and to meet up with that person—Kristen—who saw my interest was piqued and encouraged that.

I began to pray—because, finally, after a bunch of mistakes and screwups I finally began listening to the Holy Ghost and relying on His answers. After living my youth really relying on myself, mostly because the guidance and wisdom of adults around me was lacking or unavailable, it was hard to let go of control—it still is. But God. You're going to hear that phrase so many times. It really took what feels like a shameful amount for God to get ahold of not just my heart but my will. OK, back to the story…so I started praying in earnest for direction and for His will. God began to open doors and rearrange my work schedule and soon I was in nursing school. Terrified? Yup. Straight up. This was me, at 26, going back to school again. There were pitfalls along the way to be sure. School turned out to be one of the "easy" things, to be honest. I had been a home health aide and a phlebotomist along with a microbiology tech for years now, so some of the basic things weren't bad.

One big thing that happened along the way was my first pregnancy. Want to talk about praying?? Whew. I was on the fence as it was about kids—what in the name of all that's holy did I know about raising kids without traumatizing them? Jack diddly squat. Nada. In my mind I had a long list of what not to do, but the thought of being responsible for raising a tiny human being without feeling I would destroy them was terrifying. We were not trying to start a family—especially not then! Indeed, we were trying NOT to. But God does have His reasons and His timing. Friends, I struggled so. Very. Hard. With. This! At this point, I had started going to my current church with Kristen (more grace!!!) and I was learning more to pray and trust. Finally, when I hit around my ten-week mark, I felt peace about this baby. It would work out. God had allowed this child and it would be OK! Week twelve, I began cramping in clinicals (I was around a year into the nursing program); when I got home, I was having some bleeding. I called the doctor who, though sympathetic, told me I would have to wait things out. Next day things worsened and then the pains started to hit. You guys, I thought I had a good pain tolerance—boy howdy, I was so wrong. I knew I was going to lose this baby. We headed to the hospital, and I had an ultrasound done. My ladies out there—talk about insult to injury. You're already hurting and then…well, I won't get descriptive. The baby was already gone—nothing had passed yet but there was no baby visible, just streaking. By this point, I was in so much pain I was physically sick. The decision was made to take me to the OR and do a D&E to allow my body to heal.

Several things occurred in a short span of time, and they were all evidence of grace, even though at the time I didn't think so. First, I learned a lesson in what not to say to a hurting, grieving woman who is losing or has lost her baby to miscarriage. Do not EVER say you can get pregnant again. I looked at the nurse who told me this as I was now sobbing in pain, both emotional and physical, and said, "Are you sure? How do you know?" She had no answer to that. Second, I found out just how sensitive my body is to meds. Now, that doesn't seem like grace, does it? Sure didn't feel that way at the time or the next few hours but it would prove to be God showing grace in the revealing later. The first med they gave me was one called Toradol—it's really a great med—to help with pain. I was not aware that it is an NSAID (nonsteroidal anti-inflammatory), and it is chemically similar to aspirin. Not everyone with an aspirin allergy is allergic to NSAIDs but some are—guess who is one? Yup! ME!! The other med was Fentanyl—we use it for pain in the ICU in small doses and sometimes as a continuous drip for pain and sedation with certain patients, but it is also given to help induce anesthesia. Well, for me it induced hallucinations. To make things better, the Toradol didn't help my pain at all. The Fentanyl did but it also made the sink spin and turn itself on. Weird, bad feeling but highly entertaining for my hubby and Kristen. Bless that woman, she has seen me at my worst!! I woke up after surgery, sore and knowing that I had lost my baby, and the vomiting began. When there wasn't anything left the dry heaving began. For six solid hours, I had the most intense ab workout as I dry heaved that entire time without relief.

I know what you're thinking—actually I don't have a clue what's going through your mind, but I know what I'm thinking. Where is grace here? Seriously, this is all bad. The beauty of this book? It's retrospective. Man, I didn't see grace in that moment fo sho—I was hurting, grieving, and dry heaving. Let me take a minute and be thankful for all that—NOT! But here is where God allowing what seems like terrible circumstances can be for our good and His glory. If I had not lost that baby, I may never have yearned so deeply to be a mom. My heart had been awakened to a love only a mother knows. After that, I was eager to start a family—I wanted a baby! We did wait, and I am so grateful for the healing grace God gave there and awakened a yearning only He could give. The meds? Let's just say after many more surgeries, I am so picky about what I will let them give me—and believe me I make them tell me everything they are hitting me with. Every. Thing. That grace He extended protected my body from meds He knew would harm me—I am convinced of this. Truly, in the loss of that child who I will see again one day my relationship with my husband and my best friend Kristen deepened considerably!

Six months from the end of finishing nursing school! I was getting excited—new career, more time for myself, with friends and family—it was in sight! At this point I was working 36 hours a week on the weekends (Thursday through Saturday nights) and in clinicals four days a week. I was, quite literally, at the hospital every day for four months!! As

God would deem it, I got pregnant again. This time, I was thankful from the beginning and prayed earnestly for a healthy pregnancy! Talk about grace—I was exhausted. Absolutely done in. It was a relatively healthy pregnancy, but I had three ear/sinus infections and my blood pressure started creeping up around my 24-week mark. I was determined to finish even with that—again, the end was in sight!! My body was mentally and physically exhausted. I relied on prayer very heavily—I'm fairly certain I prayed from the minute my feet hit the floor until I went to bed at night. I also learned to cry—sounds crazy, doesn't it? I mean, we all know how to cry—but I had gotten to the point where I didn't allow myself to cry. I had been conditioned in my childhood to think that crying was bad, it meant I was weak, it wouldn't do me any good to cry…well anyways. Crying in my family drew negative attention and anger from my mom, so I just stopped crying.

Unfortunately (fortunately, I guess? Maybe?) when you're pregnant you pretty much can't help crying. It's a given. Can I get an amen from my mamas out there?? I cried all. The. Time. Oh my word. It got to be laughably ridiculous. Nature shows? Cried. The national anthem playing at the Olympics that year? Sobbed. Wow. I was ten weeks pregnant when 9/11 happened. What a horrible, how could God allow this mess! But He did allow it, like many other things that seem awful and uncontrollable. Could I even begin to fathom a reason why? No—I am not God. What 9/11 awakened in me was a closer dependence on Him and a recognition of His sovereignty. I cannot speak for anyone else, but the stark fear I felt that day, especially when Pennsylvania got hit, was overwhelming. My parents actually lived 100 feet from the entrance of a nuclear power station!! But here is another moment of grace—just a speck of knowledge. I had taken care of someone while I was a home health aide—he "just happened" to work on building nuclear reactors safe from…you guessed it…plane wrecks. What?? I'm guessing that "chatter" had already been heard that this was a possibility and I learned that the modern reactors were built low to the ground and partially underground with six feet thick rebarred concrete walls to prevent being destroyed from being hit by a plane. Wow!! (I have no clue if this is true everywhere, just my little section of Pennsylvania, and no I haven't formally researched it—I just remembered later what he had told me!) I had a new realization of just how short life can be; how much of a witness we need to be, because we just never know when Jesus will call us home! I experienced that day the grace of my family's protection up in Pennsylvania.

December 2001, I received my associates degree in nursing. In January 2002 I took and passed the NCLEX. (Nursing boards—meant I was legal to practice!) My baby was due March 25, 2002. By December, my legs had started swelling terribly. By the end of January, I had developed something called PIH (pregnancy induced hypertension); by the end of February, I had developed preeclampsia. I was put on modified bed rest the first day of March. Go me—my body was finally getting a chance to REST!! Problem? Boredom. I was so used to being on the go constantly; this only got worse the past two years!!

My doctor did tell me I could walk to the mailbox and back and do a little housework—like do a few dishes, fold clothes, make a meal—but that was it. Yay!! First week of March I walked out to the mailbox; my neighbor was burning something. I found out the next day it was poison oak, which was rampant in our area. Now, up north we had poison ivy and sumac (which I'm very reactive to and had had systemic poison ivy before—fun fun!), but not poison oak. Guess what I'm highly allergic to? YAY ME!!! Free fun fact #98234779235497 about me—not only will I react to touching the leaves but also the SPORES blowing, and that's how I ended up getting this lovely case of please just kill me. I had already had systemic poison oak from contact; it got into a scratch; and I had done the steroid and bathe in calamine lotion thing, so when I saw the welts the next day after getting the mail, I knew what was happening and called my doc. They put me on a Medrol pack (steroids) on March 9th. I started spotting the next day. We went to the hospital, and I was spilling protein into my urine from the preeclampsia, so they decided to keep and watch me. My blood pressure was also stupid high. Bad, nasty high.

By morning I was wretched. I had poison oak covering both arms, chest, abdomen, and upper thighs. I hadn't slept thanks to the steroids and oh by the way I WAS in labor. I didn't even register that because the poison oak had me in such pain. Grace? I don't know. Seriously. I was so miserable I couldn't tell you. I couldn't have anything to eat or drink—not even Tylenol for pain. They decided to induce me—oh joy. The only clear spot they could get an IV in was between my knuckles, so there it went. And then they started the Pitocin.

Let me pause and tell you a little about Pit. It is nicknamed Pit, and after experiencing it firsthand I can tell you it is straight from the pit. Pit of despair, pit of agony—that'll work. It causes contractions to come faster and harder, so the joys of labor are intensified!! Oh joy!! (If no one has picked up by now, I am very sarcastic!) I couldn't get any IV pain medicine, so after four hours of brutality I broke down and got the epidural. I HATE my back messed with (and yes, that will come back later in the book) but oh was I thankful for pain relief!! For those who know my full labor story with Kaitlyn and what a sweet and gentle demon I turned into (steroids + no sleep + pain + pit = bad, bad Mel!!)—when they called in the charge nurse, I knew I may possibly have crossed a line. You see, charge nurses get called in when there is a complaint, or someone is behaving badly. I was of the latter camp.

But even there, there was grace!! HOW??? This sweet nurse was an older lady with a lot of experience pulling laboring and birthing mamas off the ceiling, so to speak. The nurse turning up the Pit wasn't so nice. I won't tell you what she said but let's just say she was less than sympathetic to my plight. This dear sweet woman, this charge nurse—I know God sent in to calm me and be a substitute mama. She just kept working with me calmly and started prepping me for delivery as she went. She was a calm in the storm. My hubby wasn't so calm—he was ready to go after the other nurse! (Oops!!)

Around an hour after my epidural and five minutes of pushing my beautiful daughter, Kaitlyn Leigh, was born. She was 9 lbs, 21 ¾ inches long and 15 days early. Bless the Lord for His grace in allowing an early delivery—that child would have been at least 10 lbs if not!! She was healthy with great lungs and was so beautiful with a head full of black hair; she looked like a little sumo wrestler! I couldn't do skin to skin because of the poison oak, but I got to hold and cuddle my gift from God. Kaitlyn Leigh means "pure meadow" but Leigh can also mean "healer". Little did I know how true in many ways her name would turn out to be! God's grace shone strong the day she was born. So many things could have gone wrong with my delivering her so sick, but God protected me again and again!!

Two days after I had Kaitlyn, I was able to go home! One bad thing from being in the hospital—I picked up a secondary bacterial infection that followed the tract of my poison oak called nummular eczema. If you could have lit my nerve endings on fire, I can't imagine the pain could have been worse. A week after I had Kaitlyn and during that time basically no sleep and being on steroids, my husband packaged up a wife nearly weeping with exhaustion AND a newborn and drove us to the doctor's office. No one, until we got to the office, knew what this weird fiery red rash was that had developed! In typical God fashion of "putting people in the way", my nurse practitioner knew what it was as soon as she saw it. Commence to round of steroids #2 including a shot of steroids in the arm and an antibiotic shot in the other arm; also, another Medrol pack and oral antibiotics plus meds to help with the itching. Off we went!

Quick insert here. If you've never taken steroids, be thankful. It's miserable. Emotional lability, crying jags, keep the knives so I don't kill anyone, and hey let's not sleep for more than an hour at a time. WHOA. Am I ever grateful for the calming, even keeled presence of my husband during this time! I couldn't take care of myself, much less a newborn baby. My dreams of breastfeeding were gone—I was just too sick. I was exhausted, emotional, and feeling like a failure—it was really, really hard. I would hear Kaitlyn cry and then I would cry and beg God for mercy. We didn't have much family nearby and we lived 40 minutes from my church; we just didn't have much support. Thank God for Kristen; she came almost every day after work for a few minutes just to check on me! The fog lifted after a week or so after the next round of meds. God's grace indeed supported me. I was too exhausted to pray but this is where the intervention of Godly friends came in! When you are in a bad place, make sure those surrounding you are willing to hold up your hands spiritually as Moses's hands were held up physically!! God's grace and answers to prayer will indeed come through the intervention of others bearing your burdens—I will attest to this time and again!

Let me backtrack for a minute and now tell you how we came to be at my church!! Folks, if you have been reading this as a Christian and you don't have a local church to fellowship with, let me encourage you—no, urge you—to find one!! I am not saying my church is perfect because we sure aren't. The people aren't perfect. Our pastor isn't perfect. But for me, it's perfect.

In a funny story, I introduced Kristen to Josh (funny because there are no coincidences with God—He has His hand on all things, even when we can't see what's going on!). Kristen was a nurse in CVICU at the time; I worked in the lab, and Josh worked in CCU. In my job, I literally walked all over the hospital, so I met, well, everybody. I mean, errrryyybody. Kristen was being hounded pretty persistently by another hospital employee to go out with him. She had no interest and had nicely expressed this, but he just wouldn't give up. She didn't want to hurt his feelings either. A plan was born; I asked Josh if he would mind being a "deflection" for Kristen. (Hey, we didn't lie about the situation!) He agreed. The two met up in the lab where I worked. Kristen was off work and got herself a little gussied up to meet him—she is a gorgeous woman, so the gussying up equated to completely stunning! Josh came up to the lab (he was working) to meet her and he was a little stunned.

The plan was not for Kristen and Josh to really date, but he did end up asking her out. The three of us had all attended Bob Jones; Josh's family was very active in a local church. Kristen and I hadn't settled into one yet. We had both visited some churches, but nothing had a good "fit." There is some Holy Ghost here—I had been praying for a good church, the right church—but hadn't found it yet. God sent the Holy Ghost as a Comforter to us and to bring things to our remembrance, and Jesus promised He would give us peace. In James 1:5 it says, "If any man lack wisdom, let him ask of God, who giveth to all men liberally, and upbraideth not; and it shall be given him." If you are seeking to do what God wants you to do—and we are told to be in fellowship with our fellow believers—God will lead you to the right place!

Kristen went to church with Josh, and she in turn invited me. Background: I came from a small, quiet, conservative independent fundamental Bible believing church in Pennsylvania. It was not a loud worshipping church. It was not a hand raising church. And may I add, there is nothing wrong with that!! That small church was where I grew in Christ, learned a lot of Bible, and saw the demonstration of the love of God over and over again. It was just different. Then I went to Bob Jones—big place, quiet conservative worship. Temple Baptist Church is NOT that way, and initially it terrified me! My first visit was during Jubilee—our revival services—and as is said down South, it got on like Donkey Kong!! Hand raising, praying, people at the altars praying—there was a freedom of worship such as I have never experienced. Is it for everyone? Nope. Is it for me? YES!

What drew me so quickly was the choir. I love music and love singing, in case you haven't picked up on that! The Holy Spirit ministers to my heart in music every day. Not everyone is like that, and it is totally OK—we are all different! The expressions on the faces of the choir members as they sang and worshipped was beautiful! It felt like home! There is nothing chance with God—we might not see what He is doing, but God orchestrated me to find my church home at that time! God knew long before I ever set foot in that place what help and fellowship I would get over these 20 years worshipping at Temple Baptist. It amazes me to think how He placed me in such a place as He has. I marvel at the people I have been blessed to meet, the connections only God could see the need for 20 years down the road, the lessons He has taught me! How He has opened my eyes to be able to look back and see how His grace, at so many times unrecognized, was weaving a golden thread through the tapestry of my life. May I praise Him always for His unmerited favor!

As I look back on how God placed me at my church (which, on reflection, I actually was praying for—but I honestly don't feel like I knew how to pray well at this time!) and I'm just in awe. It's helping remind me even now, experiencing things with this season of Covid, how He will continue to work all things for our good (Romans 8:28). Friends, our "good" and God's "good" doesn't always look the same. Our "good" tends to seem like we will prosper with finances, with relationships, and filled in a never-ending circle of peace, sunshine, and happiness. (Once again, please note the sarcasm!) For many years I felt like this is how God would work things for my good.

But what, really, is for my good? My good, as a Christian, is to become more like Jesus! The very definition of Christian is to be like Christ! It is to be a reflection of Jesus to the world around me. One of my brother's favorite verses is John 3:30—"He must increase, but I must decrease." John 12:32 says, "And I (Jesus), if I be lifted up from the earth, will draw all men unto me." Being more like Jesus, many times, will involve suffering on our part—but how much did Jesus suffer, leaving heaven willingly to be born as an infant? He was helpless except for His parents and yet was He aware of the entire road before Him? Of course He was—He is God! He became man but was still fully God! And yet He came, and He willingly humbled Himself and became "obedient unto death, even the death of the cross" (Philippians 2:8). Philippians 3:10a states "That I may know Him, and the power of his resurrection, and the fellowship of his sufferings." Personally, I can't find another way around this verse but to know Jesus, we will at some point suffer with Him; but we are never alone in them because He is in fellowship with us during those times!

Would I have really seen and known my Savior, experienced the richness and fulness of His grace to the extent I have, if life had always been perfect and easy? I would not. My deepest moments of pain, when I have so many times cried out in desperation to Jesus, is when I have felt His presence the most deeply. Do I, as a finite little being who cannot comprehend the "whys" of life, fight against those hard times and still ask why? YES! Absolutely yes, because sometimes, many times, faith is hard. Walking in blind faith can sometimes feel like fear but it is the most freeing thing, knowing that giving up control of something to Jesus means I don't have to worry about it anymore! Now—repeat that to yourself about a million times over, just like I will!

I will be totally and completely honest here: one of the hardest things for me to do is look back and realize that God did work out so many things for my good—but at the price of going through some dark valleys and incredibly trying times. I won't lie for a second and tell you I yearn for the next valley. I tend to be pessimistic; I can snatch a silver lining out and put in some thunderheads before you can blink an eye. That is not how I am supposed to be because indeed in Jesus I have hope! Does that hope mean my bills are going to be all gone tomorrow and I'll never face moments of want? Nope. It does mean that God will not allow the righteous to be forsaken nor begging for bread (Psalm 37:25, paraphrasing mine). Does that hope mean I will never again experience pain or sickness? Absolutely not—we are living in a broken, sin filled world and our bodies are breaking down! But when we experience that pain, we aren't alone. The same Savior that bled and died for me on Calvary will be with me through that pain! And oh, the blessing of feeling relief from the pain! If the God of the universe arrayed the lilies, how can I doubt that He will not provide for my needs? I can't tell you how many times as I was writing this book it struck me just what God has done in my life and how He has changed me for the better; how He has molded me and made me softer, kinder, and more compassionate. Only grace and mercy could do those things!

Point of reflection: How has your family or a family situation been impacted by grace? I know I've written much about my family in this book—I chose to insert this here because this was the beginning of MY little family with my kids. Is there a time you can remember and know that your family came through a traumatic time, times of want or need, or even a long-standing issue that you feel like you would have fallen apart except for grace?

Joshua 1:9 states, "Have not I commanded thee? Be strong and of a good courage; be not afraid, neither be thou dismayed; for the Lord thy God is with thee whithersoever thou goest."

I Peter 5:10—"But the God of all grace, who hath called us unto his eternal glory by Christ Jesus, after that ye have suffered a while, make you perfect, stablish, strengthen, settle you."

CHAPTER TEN

Darkness Descends

I STRUGGLED WITH the title of this chapter. I will, without a doubt, struggle mightily writing parts of it. This chapter will have moments of joy—they may seem brief; so many things changed, but still God enveloped me in His grace!

My mom's road to addiction and eventually her death began before Kaitlyn was born. A short synopsis: she never was taken to the dentist as a child, and by age 14 she wouldn't smile showing her teeth. By the time she had me at age 28, many of her teeth had been pulled. I remember her frequent dentist visits; strangely, she never complained much of physical pain—she had been dealt many physically terrible blows in her life, so I'm just guessing it was accepted to her. She wouldn't talk about it. One thing I inherited from her was being very sensitive to meds. She couldn't tolerate Advil or the like, so it was Tylenol or bust. She always had Vicodin (a strong prescription narcotic) sitting around because of her dental work.

I honestly don't remember her taking those pain pills much. Over the years, she had been prescribed different meds for anxiety, etc (I don't know which ones) but she never consistently took them, or she would attempt to overdose on them. After she accepted Jesus as her Savior when I was 12, she really did much better emotionally and psychologically and didn't take anything at all for a long time. Something happened, though, when I was in my 20's and not living at home anymore. She had a terrible headache and had already taken Tylenol without relief, so she took half of a Vicodin. (I honestly think her headaches were anxiety driven—just my opinion!) Something changed after she took it. In one of our rare open talks, she told me later that she felt amazing after taking the Vicodin. And so, the journey began. Half a pill became one, then two, then six in the morning with coffee before work so she could work. Again, I was living in South Carolina now and only seeing the edges of the problem.

So here is the thing with addiction. I can tell you from my mom's story that it wasn't a path she intended. One pill, one day, made that difference. Addiction steals from the person and everyone around them. Prior to this, as I said, my mom had been doing better emotionally and psychologically than she ever had. She was going to Bible study. She had finally started to form friendships with some ladies from church. Addiction slowly ate away at that. She pushed my dad to give her his pain pills (he had terrible back problems and was prescribed the same meds) and to refill scripts even when she didn't need them. There were other things that happened that I won't elaborate on; let me simply say that it is a dark, lonely place to be in, knowing that I couldn't help my mom—only God could.

She finally admitted she had a problem before my girls were born. It was a relief…an answer to prayer…a gift from God—truly grace from above! I wish she had sought professional help, Christian counseling, something—I honestly believe she was afraid of uncovering and dealing with years of pain she had never resolved. What ended up happening is she was placed on meds for anxiety, which she needed all along—and let me insert this here—there is NOTHING wrong with needing help! NOTHING wrong with needing meds. Our brains are an organ and can be affected by disease like our heart and lungs; if you don't treat the disease, it could eventually destroy you.

I wish—I have always wished—that my dad would have helped my mom heal instead of just giving in so she would be "quiet." So many arguments he just sat there and let her scream at him and berate him, and the points she argued just weren't true—they were projections, many times, of what her father or some other male figure had done to her, or she had seen done. He didn't dispute her. I, on the other hand, began to dispute—and this should shock exactly NO ONE who knows me. When I pointed out during one particularly frustrating argument with her it was in the encyclopedia, going so far as to point it out to her, she said the encyclopedia was wrong!! I threw the book down and walked away!!

Her last suicide attempt was after she had had a stroke and then showered clot to her optic nerve, leaving her barely able to speak and blind in one eye. I believe it was in 2004; Erica (my middle child) was close to a year old. She took almost a whole bottle of my dad's muscle relaxants. My dad found her unresponsive and called 911; she seized in the ER and they intubated her and put her on a vent. Along with the physical and mental pain, she was prone to terrible bouts of pneumonia (being a three to four pack per day smoker) and colds/flu. She had gotten pneumonia as well. Flying up and seeing her on the vent was a strange disconnect being a critical care nurse.

She was removed from the vent and one of the nurses developed some kind of rapport with her. I can see it, truly—there were times she could be absolutely hilarious. I'm not sure what transcribed that night she opened up to this nurse (and I've had similar situations with patients—WOW, that is a lot of trust folks give us, and I don't take it lightly!!)—but my mom unburdened herself to this night shift nurse. Can I give you a hint? It's hard to rattle us. I've had patients tell me stories that had me sobbing later on. We have seen things we can't unsee. But this nurse, bless her, insisted on a psych consult. None of my family would talk to the psychiatrist. My dad thought she would get the "third degree", no matter how many times I told him they only wanted to help. We had all spent our lives trying to "quiet" mom but only succeeded in making matters worse. My hand shot up this time, though—this felt like my last time to try to help her! I talked to the psychiatrist for a long time. I am so grateful for that kind lady who sat and listened; I believe if given the chance she would have done everything she could to help.

Since mom was in the hospital for a suicide attempt, she was on involuntary commitment—in Pennsylvania that meant a three-day minimum stay (at least at that time). She should have gone to an inpatient facility, but my dad signed her out against medical advice—sigh. I know in his heart he wanted to protect her from more "hurt." I still wish he had let her get help. She went back home, angry at my dad for letting her get intubated (I tried to warn him—did he believe me? NOOO…), and now on meds for seizures. There were times it was hard to see God's grace in this, but He did allow for three more years with family and to see her 60th birthday. He allowed her to make peace with some things; He allowed me the directness to ask her if she knew for certain that she was saved. I also asked at that time if she ever wanted to be put on a vent again—I felt like I knew that answer but wanted to make sure we knew her wishes. Hard questions—but God still shows up, in that whispered prayer of "God give me this moment" or "give me strength." I know He hears our groanings which we can't utter because it is promised that the Holy Spirit will do that for us (Romans 8:26)—I am beyond thankful that God in His mercy and grace sent us a Comforter to us for that, because I can't tell you how many times "help me" or "Jesus" has been the only thing I could utter in prayer.

The year prior to this, in contrast to the darkness and despair of this time, we had my second daughter, Erica Danielle. She and Kaitlyn are only 20 months apart. I am so grateful God allowed me to have a much easier pregnancy and delivery than with Kaitlyn! Mild joint pain; mild blood pressure issues. Possibly the hardest moment carrying her was the last shift I worked—I ended up being the only nurse available to pull one of our huge crash carts into a room! Honestly after that, it looked like I had been riding a horse for days with every step I took! She was another big, beautiful baby—all 9 lbs 9ozs of her! (And she was a week early!) Her labor and delivery were blissfully anticlimactic, praise Jesus! Her name means "ruler" and "God is my judge"; she surely has been a different, independent, feisty spirit! As a baby and toddler, she was so full of smiles and laughs! God surely looked down with grace and blessed us with such a sweet, pleasant baby to balance out the issues with my family and those to come with Kaitlyn!

Isn't that just like our Father? There is never just one thing going on in life—oh no. That's just not how it goes. I'll say now—the next chapter will deal with my oldest daughter's autism diagnosis that we were wading through at that time. I promise, it deserves its own chapter. Maybe even a full book one day, but I digress. Here we are, dealing with a child who we KNOW something has changed (I've been fussed at before when I said something was "wrong" with her, but whatever)—fighting docs every step of the way—and dealing with my mom and her many issues on top of that. In the middle of this, we have our sweet, happy little baby showcasing God's grace and lightening the load. There were so many hard times, but so many sweet memories—I love looking back at her baby pictures and seeing her smile. I'm also so thankful my mom got to hold Erica; for all her faults, she adored being a grandma and she was good at it.

The irony of Erica? My 9 lb 9 oz baby is now a tiny, petite, 5 foot tall 100 lbs soaking wet little 18-year-old. She remains sweet natured but is now quiet and reserved (until she knows you really well!) but is sweet, loving, and caring. She knows how to pray. She and I don't listen to the same music, but we love the same Jesus; while I am loud, (obnoxiously so) brash (bossy? I say assertive but whatever!!), and just a little over the top sometimes, she is quiet and gentle. I love talking to people; she just loves people without talking to them. I'm a hugger; she comes and asks for hugs when she is ready (I'm fairly certain she might be part cat.).

She loves art and drawing; I'm pretty much a give me the pattern kinda gal and I'll make that but don't ask me to just design something on my own—as much as I am left brained, she is definitely right brained! As different as we are, she truly has a heart of gold!

I'm including some stories about my last two pregnancies in this chapter because, well…I can't quite get them to fit anywhere else, but there sure is grace involved; there were some moments of darkness here, as well.

When Erica was around two years old, I got pregnant again. This pregnancy was odd—I never felt good about it. Around six weeks along, I suddenly felt better; this should have been a big tip off. Eight weeks, I went in for a routine ultrasound. I was looking at the screen, and immediately noticed that there was no little heartbeat on the screen. The tech was very, very quiet as she looked. I asked—she said no, there was no heartbeat. But I noticed something else…on the side of the screen there was pulsatile flow.

Pulsatile on an ultrasound usually deals with blood flow. I knew something was really wrong.

I asked the tech what was going on on that side—she said she needed to get the doc. Off she went—and me still just lying there knowing I had lost this baby but something else was wrong. The doctor came in and gently explained about the baby being gone. Hard enough, but then about the other…he couldn't clearly tell me what was going on there. We discussed doing a D&E; I pushed for it because I knew deep down something was so wrong.

That very evening, I went in for another surgery—this was my second D&E. So grace…grace came in here because I knew this anesthesiologist. He dropped our hearts off to us pretty often, so he knew me. Whew. You never realize how much you want to see a familiar face until a moment like that!! More grace: he LISTENED. When I explained about my earlier med issues he really listened, and he loaded me up so I wouldn't get sick on top of everything.

The procedure went well, as well as could be expected…then I found out the next day that it was a molar pregnancy. What that means is it could be cancerous—it's an overgrowth, basically, and it takes over the normal pregnancy. That explained everything—and I'm so thankful I noticed that weird flow, much less knew it was off! And here is the next moment of mercy and grace: it resolved. Many times, with a molar pregnancy women will have to take basically chemo drugs to make sure nothing is growing abnormally. For someone who can't take aspirin, the thought of a chemo drug is just a bit scary.

Man, did I pray…and praise God, He answered my prayers; I didn't have to take anything. Hallelujah!! One more week with high hormone levels and I would have had to take some strong meds. I was so thankful!!

So how can I possibly say there is grace there?

Knowing God is orchestrating EVERYTHING. Down to knowing the doc putting me to sleep. When I got back to work, he dropped one of my surgery patients off and gave me a big hug. Knowing God is watching out for little old me, this little speck of a person on this planet…knowing He knows me better than I know myself and protecting me from having to take those meds. Wow. I don't deserve for Him to love and protect me that way!!

My last pregnancy was my daughter Natalie—otherwise known as Nat, or Newt, or Nat Nat…you get the idea. Natalie means "the Lord's birthday" and her middle name is Ann, which was my mom's middle name. Ann means "favour" or "grace"—ironic, since I had never looked that up! I wanted her to have that name in honor of my mom, the grandmother she won't meet until Heaven. Honestly, her pregnancy was the easiest—it's like God looked down and said, I'm pretty sure Mel is done and needs something to rejoice in. Ha!! Nat was born in 2009, about a year and a half after my mom died. With her pregnancy, I failed my one-hour glucose tolerance test (oh yay!), but thankfully my OB doc was completely fine with me carb counting until I could take my three-hour test. I noticed I felt better once I was counting carbs! I passed my three-hour test without problems. Nat turned out to be my smallest child; this leads me to believe that maybe I developed gestational diabetes sometime after being tested with my other two babies.

Nat was an easy delivery as well—one push and she blew into this world! She was only 8 pounds, 5 ounces—seriously, she was a midget compared to my other girls. Ha!! What did I learn about grace at this time? Well, first—the gestational diabetes part. Little did I know then how much I would lean on counting carbs later!! Hallelujah for reading labels and nutrition class!! God in His mercy was "prepping" me for later! More grace? An easy delivery—seriously, no bad moments, some pain—and healed quickly. That also allowed me to be home and study for a certification test which has helped me so tremendously as a critical care nurse! (Yes…this nurse studied whilst recovering from childbirth—you're welcome.)

More grace…my mom had already passed by the time Nat was born. I have rose pedals in my Bible from her memorial service; when I opened my Bible the first time to read while I was in the hospital, lo and behold rose petals fell out. I sobbed, knowing my mom wouldn't meet Nat on earth; my mom LOVED being a grandma. But those rose petals…were they God's way of saying mom was ok in heaven? I would like to think they were a little whiff of grace letting me know my Father was reassuring me that all was well.

The last part of this chapter will deal with my mom's death. This is a hard section with many emotions that I could drag into it—I feel like I have to include some, but I want the focus to be on God's grace because there was so much of it showered through this time.

My mom's docs put her on meds to help with her anxiety and now uncovered chronic pain and sleep issues. In the long list of "I wishisms," I wish I had been able to break away and check on her more often in person. Dealing with working 48-60 hours/week plus having two small children, one of whom we were now navigating the complex world of special needs, just didn't allow it. I remember calling my dad frequently, usually every day, in the two to three weeks before her death. She seemed to always be sleeping; I relayed my concerns to my brother since he only lived ten minutes away. One day he called me and told me I needed to come up and say goodbye.

On the plane ride up to Pennsylvania, I remember just feeling overwhelmingly sad. I knew how my mom had suffered, especially just in the last three years. I didn't want her suffering to be prolonged. That teetering point between no I don't want her to die but please Lord, don't let her suffer overlong! When I got up there, my mom was horribly disoriented, and my dad was exhausted. But even here—so much grace! He had no idea who to turn to for help. He just wouldn't call my brother and ask for help; he was a stubborn old mule who could just manage himself! I called my brother and sisters; as it turns out my sister knew someone who worked with the state who went out of his way to see my parents as soon as possible—she called Tuesday and he was there Wednesday!! Now again, I'll say—I don't believe in coincidences. God knew that man was there! He played a small but mighty role in our family that week! On Wednesday, my sister-in-law had emergency surgery. My nieces and nephews at the time were still grade school and early teens. I'm thankful God in His providence allowed me to be there to stay with them so my brother could be at the hospital with her! We had a great time that night despite the circumstances; I don't get to see them nearly enough!

I treasured two of those days up there where I was able to cook some of my mom's favorite foods and she ate well. She hadn't been eating much at all; she had pressure ulcers on her head and other places. I did my best to reorient her, and we watched old movies together. She couldn't speak well, but she cried and allowed me to take care of her. Being a nurse, I was able to judge her fatigue pretty quickly, help her to the bathroom, and just sit with her. Another example of God's grace—not only allowing me that time but placing me "in the way" where He could use me to help. Thursday came; I had to get back to South Carolina. My oldest was five years old; she had been formally diagnosed with autism two years prior and was getting extensive in-home therapy. My youngest at the time was three and a half. I am beyond thankful for a husband who never complained about the extra work and for coworkers who dropped off food and checked in on them. More grace! God truly gives more than we can ever know!

My nieces and nephews begged me to stay Thursday night. They wanted me to go roller skating with them. Did I want to? Absolutely! But I knew in my heart I had to head back. Little did I know the role of grace in that moment…Thursday at 11am was the last time I would see my mom on this earth. I already knew this was goodbye here—not only as a daughter seeing her mom this sick, but as a nurse we know when death is near. As I was giving my mom one last long hug, my brother was behind me. Bless him, I fussed at him for this next moment—he told my mom, even though I had warned him not to, that I would be up in August. I didn't want my mom to feel pressure to fight to stay alive another three weeks—and I have seen that very thing happen before. This was July 19th, and after watching my mom for a few days I knew she was going to meet Jesus within the next few days. I leaned over to mom and told her, "I love you, Mom—be at peace and I will see you later." My brother and I drove off to the airport with my mom crying. I called her at 7pm when I finally landed in Greenville. She was the clearest she had been all week. I asked her how her day had been; she said it was good. After a week of her being very anxious and crying jags, she was very calm. I told her again I loved her, and that I wanted her to be okay with going to heaven whenever Jesus called her. Another moment of thankfulness for God's grace, that He gave her that last day on earth to be good and for her to be mentally clear. What a gift and what grace!!

The next morning at 9am, I got the phone call that would flip our worlds upside down. Friends—it doesn't matter how close or distant you are from your parents. When you get "that call"—it will be shocking. My brother called and said, "Mel, she's gone—mom's gone. The house is gone." I remember yelling mom, and then hitting my knees in our laundry room where I had been pulling clothes from the dryer. Franky knew right away. We had no idea where my dad was or if he was alive. Remember the man who came to help coordinate my mom's care that my sister knew? The one who was at the house on Wednesday? Turns out he "just so happened" to be watching the early news, and "just happened" to see the six-alarm fire on the local news. He knew it was my parents' house—he had just been there! He also "just happened" to know my sister-in-law's brother William, who was a farmer. He called William, who called my sister-in-law Kathryn. She called my brother at work—she just said you need to go check on your parents—now. Brian drove over, not having any idea what he was about to see. Indeed, my parents' house was just a shell.

My mom was terrible about smoking in bed, and that night at 1am, she got up and managed to light a cigarette. She was so weak it fell on her robe. My dad woke up with my mom standing in front of him on fire. He tried to put it out—wrapped her in a comforter and got her onto the bed.

It got worse from there—in the end, the fire was so hot it blew out the windows in my parents' bedroom, blew a hole through the ceiling and then through the roof, and proceeded to tear through the house.

So again—where is grace here, you ask? How can I find grace in this moment? The first moment, beyond the circumstances of finding out from family instead of a police officer, was God compelling me to go back to South Carolina. I wanted, for a few moments, to stay and spend one more night with my nieces and nephews—it had been a grueling, mentally and emotionally exhausting week. The thought of roller skating was awesome. But I felt compelled to go home—almost driven. I knew Franky had the girls well in his care, but I needed to GO. If I hadn't left, I feel very certain I would have died in the fire. It blew through the house—it was an older home with plenty of accelerant (old glue from wallpaper, carpeting, etc), and because it was made of cement block and stucco it heated up like an oven, according to the fire examiner. So, once again, God chose to spare my life. I would have had to try to go down the steps, which would have been impossible within minutes of the fire starting. The other alternative would have been trying to get out the window off a tin roof, and that might not have worked either! But God knew!

The next moment of grace? Who survived the fire. No, my mom did not survive. My dad survived—he had to be air lifted to a burn unit and dealt with the pain of second and third-degree burns, but not nearly as extensive as they could have been. He also had to deal with some pretty bad smoke inhalation and an even worse case of survivor's guilt. He lost everything he had, physically. But in the end, he gained a new home and my stepmom, and a closeness with me that he had never had before. You see, my mom didn't allow my dad to have a relationship with us. What else survived the fire? I still get chills thinking of this next one…

Isaiah 55:1 states, "So shall my word be that goeth forth out of my mouth; it shall not return unto me void." I pray I am not taking this in any way out of context, because my understanding is that God's word, when used in the right way, will always and in some ways have benefit. In this case, I can tell you not one Bible in my parents' old home was destroyed—barely even damaged! There were several of my brother's and my old Bibles in a cedar chest in my old room. My mom's Bible, in my opinion, was the biggest miracle—it blew out her bedroom window from the heat of the fire and landed outside. There were a couple of singed pages but no significant damage! My dad's Bible was blown out the living room window—again unscathed. My baptismal certificate was even blown off the living room wall!

Would any of these being destroyed made God less God? Absolutely not. They were a symbol, to myself and my brother especially, that God still had complete control and His word is precious! The baptismal certificate was just a miracle, being a flimsy piece of paper in a home that was totally destroyed. I feel like God gave me that as a small gift. There was so much loss and devastation; the fact that God preserved that for me is precious to me.

There was more grace to be seen...

Financially, this was devastating for my dad. Honestly, it was difficult for me as well. I was the working parent—I had an extra plane ticket to buy, but praise God the August ticket I had bought transferred to the next flight I took on July 21st. They didn't even charge me anything extra when they heard the circumstances—anyone who has dealt with airlines knows that's a miracle! I didn't ask anyone for money, but someone from church gave me money for one trip and another person gave me some for the second trip. A Sunday School class at my church collected money for some necessities for my dad. The church I grew up in provided all the food for my mom's memorial service and took up money for my dad as well. A couple of my physician friends gave me money, and the bills that I thought I wouldn't be able to pay God provided for. How could I think of money at this time, you ask? Truthfully, I didn't think of myself. I knew we would be provided for. God had come through time and time again for us financially; I knew He would do it again!

When I flew back up for the second trip up north, I remember driving down to Atlanta and crying the whole way—but God. I had CDs in my car of some of my favorite singers at the time, and oh the comfort those songs gave me. I allowed myself the tears, because I knew once I landed, I would have to be strong for my dad especially, but also for the rest of the family. Gospel music has so much meaning for me and brings me so much comfort! I also knew that while some of my family was Christian, they don't "do" music like I do—so I tried to soak it all up driving to Atlanta! Even in the midst of tears, I knew such peace—my mom wasn't suffering on this earth anymore; she was complete and whole at the feet of Jesus! I had an entire church of people praying for my dad and my family!

I was staying with my brother and his family—more grace. Truly. My nieces and nephews were great kids, and they are awesome adults. I got to spend a lot of time with them that week. The plane ride was uneventful—more grace—God blessed me with clear skies so no motion sickness. Folks—in the middle of everything when a tornado seems to be swirling around you—you have to look for and see the little things; so many times, that's where I have found grace to be. It's like God is telling me, "I hear you; I see you—I know you can't pray anything more than 'Jesus,' but my Spirit is going to pray for you!" And our Father already knows what we stand in need of! We had meals provided by my old church—more grace. So many financial needs were met! So many moments and things I never prayed for, yet God met those needs, many times before we knew they were coming.

Even my dad being in a burn unit was a weird blessing and a moment of grace. Let me be honest—he did not take good care of himself. He went to the doctor when he was hurting and that's about it. He had already had back surgery and waited too long for that. "Stubborn" was his middle name and his nature! When he was in the hospital, he developed a heart rhythm issue. If he hadn't, they wouldn't have done a cardiac workup and found even more issues. For me, as a cardiac nurse, this was grace—I knew based on what his results were how it would go for him. I was also able to explain to my brother what was wrong and what to expect as he got older.

I have to tell this funny story, because humor is a show of grace for me. I probably mentioned that my mom adored Elvis—maybe did some worshipping? (You had to see my old bedroom—it was a shrine to Elvis. Sorta creepy!) Anyhoo. One day before my dad got out of the hospital, my sister and I were listening to Elvis in mom's memory on my brother's porch. Blue Suede Shoes came on. We were listening, I was singing; got to the second verse and never realized the words—you can burn my house, you can steal my car. Ummmm.... my sister turned to me and said, "Well, I guess we can't play that at her memorial"—and we just lost it. We laughed so hard we couldn't breathe. It might sound absolutely horrible to most people but what a moment that we needed.

There were other absolutely horrible moments during that week. Family drama? Yup. In spades. So. Much. Drama. Tears? Buckets of them shed. But in the middle—so much grace. So many moments. My parents used the same mechanic for over 20 years; the cars had fire damage to the paint. I called him and asked him if he would check the cars over to see if they were safe to drive, and of course I would pay him. He came over, checked them over, and refused to accept any money. He told me if we needed anything to please call; he would be happy to do whatever he could to assist my dad. One of my physician friends called me as we were about to walk into a Christian bookstore to buy a small Bible to bury my mom with. Honestly, I hadn't been able to cry except on the drive down to Atlanta. My family needed me to be strong. I figured eventually I would have time to grieve. When he called, I started sobbing. Couldn't get a sentence out. It blew my mind that he took the time in the middle of the afternoon to check on me. I kept apologizing and he just kept telling me it was okay. That doesn't sound much like grace, does it? For me it was—I needed to release that "steam valve" that had built up. Another moment before mom's memorial service came from looking through old pictures of her—I had so many memories of her being angry, crying jags, etc, but being able to see so many pictures of her where she was smiling and laughing gave me a great measure of peace. What a blessing that was!

Seeing my parents' house and the destruction—whew. I wish, sometimes, that I didn't have such a good memory—I will never forget walking through the house and seeing the damage. Any good or bad memory I had in that place was literally blazed through. Knowing God's word was preserved was a miracle; seeing the damage, though, gave a weird kind of closure. We tried, unsuccessfully, to keep my dad out of the house; after all, he had just gotten out of the hospital and lost my mom; but he needed to see it. He grew up so very poor and he needed to see if there was anything to salvage—I got that.

My mom's memorial service was beautiful; we sang her favorite songs and Elvis was playing softly. (In fact, after my mom's casket was rolled out of the building, my brother asked the pastor to say Doris had left the building in a nod to Elvis. It was weirdly well received!) The day she was buried was a clear, beautiful day. After the funeral my dad just wanted to drive out in the countryside, so we did just that. We talked for a long time but sometimes we just rode in the quiet. We listened to the radio; I sang. (I can't help it, folks!) When my dad died, turns out that there were still many things I didn't know about him. Even with that, I do treasure that car ride and those moments. That, indeed, was my heavenly Father showering grace on me and my dad.

The last moment of grace in this hard chapter—my dad survived. He very easily could have died, and I never would have gotten those moments with him. My dad struggled so badly after she died; he woke up every night seeing my mom on fire. He would call me crying because of it—and that man NEVER cried. My mom told me the only time she saw him cry was when his sister died of cancer. The relationship I never got to have with my dad while my mom was alive, I got a chance to have a shadow of. I'm so very grateful—his last years on earth were hard but I watched him gut through and survive every day. It might not have been pretty, but he showed me what it's like to just shoulder on and deal, even when you don't want to—that's life. So thankful for the many, many instances of grace through this loss.

Point of reflection: Have you ever suffered through a hard season of extreme pain and loss? Have you ever felt like you just couldn't deal with one more traumatic event or painful circumstance? I really don't know anyone who hasn't felt that way. Did you feel like God had abandoned you, turned a cold shoulder to you?

This reminds me of the story of Ruth; more specifically Naomi, her mother-in-law. Ruth 1:13b—"for it grieveth me much for your sakes that the hand of the Lord is gone out against me." Ruth 1:20-21—"And she (Naomi) said unto them, Call me not Naomi, call me Mara: for the Almighty hath dealt very bitterly with me. I went out full, and the Lord hath brought me home again empty: why then call ye me Naomi, seeing the Lord hath testified against me, and the Almighty hath afflicted me?" I actually have written in my Bible next to this verse I feel this way sometimes. God forgive me!

There were times writing this chapter bitterness swelled up even though I KNEW how much God's grace had swept over me—I ended up praying for forgiveness as I typed! Friend, I challenge you here—as hard as it is—LOOK for those moments of grace IN THE MOMENT. They are there; they will sustain you. It is promised that God will supply all our needs (Philippians 4:19, paraphrasing mine)—what we need, He will supply it, be it food, shelter, strength—He will provide!

CHAPTER ELEVEN

Grace I Never Needed Before

I WANT TO start this chapter with (yet another) song—it surely typifies this chapter. The words are simple but timely:

New Grace, Dr. Tom Hayes

All of grace is my story
All the way from earth to glory
Since by grace, He lifted me from sin and woe.
Living grace He has extended
As on Him my heart depended
And He'll give new grace when it's my time to go

There's been grace for every trial,
There's been grace for every mile,

There's been grace sufficient from His vast supply.
Grace to make my heart more tender,
Grace to love and pray for sinners,
But there'll be new grace when it's my time to die

Chorus:
Grace not yet discovered,
Grace not yet uncovered,
Grace from His bountiful store,
Grace to cross the river,
Grace to face forever.
There'll be new grace I've not needed before.

I love this song—it is such a testament of how I've experienced grace in my own life, and everyone who is saved from their sins has experienced to varying degrees! Living grace He has extended—new grace I've not needed before. Wow!! This next chapter has so far encompassed around 17 years—and it will continue until either myself or my daughter leaves this earth and enters the presence of God.

This chapter is about my daughter's and my family's journey with autism. I have been through some absolutely hellacious experiences in life, but nothing has come close to how difficult and how arduous our journey has been and continues to be. That being said, there have been SO many moments of grace, SO many blessings along the way!

I've already gone over Kaitlyn's birth, with a rather interesting delivery…. I'm not going to rehash all that; it isn't any more fun writing about all that again! There are about half a million theories on where/why/how autism comes about—not covering that either. I'll tell you what happened with us. Kaitlyn was a "normal" baby—"neurotypical" for us special needs parents. Looking back, there were signs—not with her, but seeing other family. Franky's mom looked at Kaitlyn one day after her diagnosis and said "She gets that from me"—Franky himself will tell you now he has Asperger's traits. Are autism and Asperger's the same? They both belong to a "developmental delay" umbrella, but they're called syndromes because the traits can vary from person to person. As it's said in our world, if you've met one person with autism, you've met one person with autism. They're as uniquely formed and made as anyone else!

Is there one thing I can do about our genetics? Nope. No more than I can change my allergies, my "fearfully and wonderfully made," or anyone else's. I have come, over the years, to love Psalm 139 more and more; I take immense comfort in it. Kaitlyn is just who God meant her to be, I am just who God meant me to be, and you, my reader friends, are just who God meant you to be! Are there things we need to work on daily? Sure. Are we responsible for taking care of ourselves? Yes.

OK, back on track here…at a year old, things changed—we didn't know for a couple more months, but here we are. Kaitlyn got her MMR (for those of you starting to roll your eyes, just go ahead and skip this chapter if you want—but this is our story!). Later that night, we heard some weird noises over the baby monitor. Franky and I went into her room and she was projectile vomiting. I put my hand on her and she felt like she was on fire. When we checked her temp, it hit 105 degrees—that was the top range of our baby thermometer! The nurse in me kicked in, the mom in me was really scared! (And the nurse in me was a new nurse and NOT a pediatric nurse!) We stripped off her pajamas and saw where she had gotten the shot her leg was hot, red, and swollen; at this point she was still vomiting.

We immediately called her pediatrician, and the result was "unconcerned"—I distinctly remember her saying, "Oh, this happens sometimes." We were encouraged to give her a tepid bath and some Tylenol. We never got a call back later to check on her. There was never undue concern. Now, let me back up a step here—I had read the research about the MMR and autism link. I did have some reserves about it but was overridden by our pediatrician. Was that God's way of warning me? I don't know. Sometimes I've wondered just that. Here's my personal take:

we clearly have a genetic link—Franky's mom was "learning disabled"—back when she was in school, autism was incredibly rare. I firmly believe the genetic inheritance plus the environmental link caused this. Would she have been different? Just quirky maybe? Had some traits? Honestly, it doesn't even matter because looking back and wishing things were different just doesn't help.

Two months after the MMR, Franky started to notice some changes in Kaitlyn. She was quieter, less eye contact, etc. She was less affectionate. Prior to this, she had always been a social, sweet, "huggy" baby. Four months later, her changes were more pronounced. She didn't make eye contact at all and stopped speaking. I, to my shame, went into denial. Sigh. By the time I had Erica (they are 20 months apart), the difference was remarkable to Franky; I was firmly grounded in said denial. It was the new baby; the pregnancy; anything else. ANYTHING else but autism. You see, to me, autism was a psych disorder—and having grown up with so many psych issues in my family, mentally I just couldn't handle it.

I kept mentioning to our pediatrician that something was "wrong" with Kaitlyn (judge away at the verbiage; I don't care. You can't judge me worse than I judge myself!). As per her usual self, the pediatrician didn't listen. In retrospect, I hate that I didn't push harder or change doctors! By the time she had her three-year checkup, our peds calmly looked at me and said, "She has a lot of the signs of autism, but I'm sure you knew that." Here's a moment of grace: I didn't kill her dead on the spot. (I'm kidding—well, maybe…) I swear on all that's holy, I felt a physical presence holding me in that chair preventing me from getting up—I was FILLED with rage. We had already been battling and I was spoiled for a fight!

Then the push came to get her tested. At the time, we didn't have many developmental peds docs in the area. The waiting list was close to a year, so while we waited, she was put through a battery of tests to rule out a physical cause. Lab work, EEG's, the hearing test—oh my. Horrific was an understatement. My poor child crawled half sideways off of me—I told them to stop. They tried to push back; I pushed back harder.

They used a mechanical toy—a monkey with cymbals of all the stupid things!—and to this day she cannot handle mechanical toys!! The sleep deprived EEG was miserable as well—remember, she was nonverbal, so activity and screaming are the only things she knew to do!

Here comes more grace, this time in the shape of a wonderful, sweet nurse—believe it or not, some of us are sweeter than others! Poor Kaitlyn—she had a terrible time with that one. Ever since she was diagnosed with autism, she has struggled with sleep issues. By the time the EEG was complete (they check EEG's, by the way, in case the autism symptoms are really caused by seizures), Kaitlyn was in full meltdown mode. Screaming, kicking, arching her back, the whole nine yards. I was trying to carry her out while Franky got the van. Honestly, being exhausted myself, I started crying, too. Not full sobbing hysterics—just crying for what we were going through, what life would be like. This lovely, sweet lady looked at me and said, "Let me hold her." We didn't have much help—we weren't used to having help. She insisted; for a few minutes I let this dear woman rock my child.

I've said it before and I'll repeat it again in this book I'm sure—if you can help someone, do it. If you have a chance to lend a hand, encourage someone, text someone, call them—do it. I have no idea if this lady was a Christian or not, but she embodied Jesus for that minute! Grace came that day for sure in a human form! That gift from God can be in whatever form He chooses to use!

Another human angel? Kaitlyn's EI's—early interventionalists. These folks came into our home and helped with Kaitlyn's early therapy at around three and a half years old. They helped us fill out reams of paperwork. Friends, let me tell you—I've worked in healthcare for years and that paperwork was challenging for me!! They took it in stride, helped fill out forms, told us who to call—I believe with all my heart God handpicked these ladies to guide us! We were so overwhelmed, and at that time His grace came through people guiding us and giving us the gift of their knowledge, expertise, and experience.

There have been so many times I have asked God WHY He allowed our daughter to go through all of this—and frankly, why we have had to go through all of this. In answer, there have been so many times that God has placed me or my husband in someone's path and allowed us to either help with information or even just truly empathize with someone walking in this path we have trod. That lightbulb moment would come at that point. We are all here on this earth, plodding through life together—honestly, we may as well help each other! I think of the verse about bearing one another's burdens—when you can help someone in any form, that's what we are doing!

I debated at length putting this next little blurb in the book...what I have found with writing this is if I can't get the thought out of my head to include something, it needs to go in. I'll be 100000% honest (I generally am, usually to my own detriment)—I have complained A LOT over the years about my life, and Kaitlyn's autism in particular. There's been lots of "hard" associated with it. Sometimes too much. On occasion, that complaining, I'm sure, has put people in a place to say SOMETHING that they think will help. So many times, it has... occasionally I struggled not to shrink back. Folks, if I'm complaining, I'm in a bad place—that means I've already been dwelling on it in my mind, usually for a long time. Already debated saying anything for fear of feeling judged for not being "spiritual" enough, thinking of who has something worse going on, etc. So many people said something sweet and inspiring and uplifting...but here's my one phrase that gets me: God gave her to you for a reason. Let that sink in, folks. If I turned around to someone who just got diagnosed with cancer and said, well, God gave you that cancer for a reason—or God took your spouse for a reason—or whatever really, horribly difficult thing you're facing—oh my word, would it not just cut to the core?? I KNOW God gave me my Kaitlyn for a reason. In the end, it should ultimately glorify God, correct? Hard to keep that front and center when you are in the fire, so to speak. Just some perspective there—and no one that said that to me ever meant anything hurtful, I promise—but wow that phrase always took the wind out of my sails.

Not too long after we finally had it confirmed that Kaitlyn did indeed have autism, we had the opportunity to get her started in school—and her teachers were amazing!! I'm still friends with a couple of them; others we have lost track of. Honestly, I cannot even recount how many times the grace of God was manifested through them. So many tears, so many times of their repeating "You're going to make it" or "You're going to get through this"! Truly, you just don't feel like you will make it when it's been a day that feels singed with brimstone—and days you just don't want to make it to the next day. One particular time when God just flat showed out was when we were moving from one town to another. We honestly moved to be closer to church—we were 35 miles away where we were living! In God's providence (again!), the county we moved to has some of the best services for autism compared to the county we were in—that one had some of the worst in our immediate area! Did we know this at the time? Nope. Did God know? Of course! Did He know that He was picking the house that we would still be in? Of course! WE had prayed that God would direct us to just the right house—and He did!

The couple that bought our home embodied graciousness. They came over just before closing as we were frantically trying to finish clean-ing. I am not criticizing, truly—our reality was we just didn't have a lot of help! I was simply too overwhelmed at the time to ask. Franky's parents were watching the girls as we loaded a moving van—just the two of us! I look back on that time and marvel that I didn't lose my mind—but grace!!! He kept me in peace and calm even in the turmoil! Anywho, the couple that bought our house came in, looked at us trying so hard to do some last-minute cleaning, and the wife looked at us and said, "It's ok. Please do not worry about the carpet—we're just going to pull it up!" I got teary eyed at her kindness!

Fast forward around 10 years. Kaitlyn, at this time, was in middle school. We went for an end of the year party, and I looked at her teacher and asked her if she had bought our house years ago. She looked confused until I told her our old address, then she looked shocked!! I started crying—I told her she and her husband were angels! I then told her how kind she was and recounted what she had said that day. Years later, she was graciously and kindly teaching our daughter and many other special needs kids. That is God for you—He is weaving a story, a pattern we can't see the front of many times and the back frankly looks pretty awful to us—but just like the tapestry that has to be woven strand by strand, the front, when we get a glimpse, has such beauty to it!! I wish grace had a color—if it did, I would imagine it to be a pearly silver color—enough to notice but not necessarily draw attention to.

The next moment of grace in our autism journey came when we were on an autism awareness walk. There was a table set up for a company called Brain Balance. Basically, the premise is retraining and balancing the left and right hemispheres of the brain to be more balanced. In many developmental disorders like autism, ADD, ADHD, and others, there is a marked imbalance between the two hemispheres. I spent at least 20 minutes talking to the doctor there. We took her information and went home. I was excited—this was such an answer to prayer!! And boy howdy had we started praying, finally! Kaitlyn had had years of ABA therapy (applied behavior analysis—it helped her learn the difference between hot and cold, that, no kidding, took two weeks!), PT/OT, aquatherapy, speech therapy-ugh!! ABA was useful but she had met her milestones and we were left wondering, where do we go from here?

Now I will say—I had learned to not put all my eggs in one basket by this point. We prayed—this would involve a big financial commitment out of pocket, and I was tired. We went for the initial evaluation—free! and prayed some more. We both felt this was the right direction. Did it yield exactly what we thought? Well, no. I wish it had. Brains, as it turns out, don't retrain as well as we want and since Kaitlyn had already started puberty early, she didn't have as stellar outcomes as younger kids. BUT we learned! And OH the massive thing we learned—the amazing amount of grace here—FOOD ALLERGIES.

It turned out when the allergy testing was done that Kaitlyn had 24 food sensitivities, ranging from 1+ (very mild, usually not noticeable) up to 4+ (severe). Her severe were dairy, soy, peanuts, MSG, and a couple others.

We were giving her soy milk because we knew about her dairy allergy, but the soy was making her sicker! Over time, we have tweaked and toyed with her food sensitivities. I cannot imagine what we would be dealing with now if we didn't know about them. The battle with her food allergies is ongoing—we know how she reacts, and we always have Zyrtec or Benadryl on hand. Thank You, Father, for graciously directing us! And thank You, Father, for giving me the ability to decipher food labels!!

The final thing I'll include concerning our autism journey is her journey through puberty. Oh. Holy. Moses. What. A. Bad. Time. One of the issues with autism is the meds that are sometimes used to help with behavioral control—we knew starting this journey that there could be potential effects; in medicine we use a term "risk to benefit ratio", meaning do the benefits of using the meds outweigh the risks? Her behaviors were so self-injurious when we started her on meds, we had to do something. If you've never seen a child throw themselves back onto your concrete deck and literally hear their skull whack, it's hard to imagine how severe it can be. Not only was she self-injurious, but she also got aggressive with others as well—and our other daughter was almost two years younger! She was already in various therapies, but she needed help. Unfortunately, those meds caused her to go through puberty early—and hard. It took less than a year to realize we were in for an unusually wild ride. By the time she was 12, we were seriously in trouble, especially considering my husband needed his valve repaired! (Don't worry, that story is coming!) She would get her period every three weeks and for the week preceding her period she would scream for the entire week. She also was barely sleeping, so we were barely sleeping!

What to do? Well, first—we prayed. A lot. It felt like all the time! We didn't sleep much. I snapped at everyone and everything. So grace—grace at this point came in the form of people again holding us up in prayer and encouraging us. So many people prayed for us and sent texts, encouraging words, and just let me vent!! The verse "rejoice with them that do rejoice, and weep with them that weep" (Romans 12:15) took on such special meaning during this time; and there is another example of grace for the moment. The Holy Spirit gifted me with just that verse at that time; He also sent me music and songs just when I needed a breathtaking moment! Through this, I learned a valuable lesson myself: I tend to be hard when I get tired. I don't get sympathetic sometimes—I get mean. What was God trying to teach me? At this point it was not to compare to others; not to compete with others; but when someone is weeping, hold them—pray for them—don't be like Job's friends and accuse someone of sinning or somehow think they "deserved" this. Not a one of us deserves anything of God, but He grants grace and mercy! I learned how better to extend grace and mercy to others during this time!

The next thing we did was fight. We fought hard to get Kaitlyn seen and listened to. We prayed about who to see her—honestly, I just prayed for God to lead us to who needed to see her and who could help her! And here is another moment of grace—when God teaches you when to stop fighting and just let God be God—give Him full control! It has been a terrible, rough, hard lesson for this control freak. Controlling what docs see her in subspecialties? Definitely and firmly in the hands of the Great Physician. Surprisingly, there is a peace in letting go. We found that. There is grace and peace in not having to control everything. In so doing, I allowed Him to lead fully rather than trying to work my plans. He led us to just the right doctor, who was so kind and gentle with her. Not only that she explained things so thoroughly, but also, we quickly had a plan—and a couple more diagnoses. That plan has worked fairly well—there are moments, but not lifetimes!

There have been many other battles even since puberty—daily battles—suffice to say no matter the battle, I have learned that I cannot fight them on my own! I just can't! There is so much of Kaitlyn I do not understand. What I will say without hesitation? I have always had someone fighting with me, for me, for her: I have always been able to reach out for the mercy seat and just cling to knowing that the suffering we endure now is going to cause us to be steadfast, established, stronger, and more settled (I Peter 5:10); eventually the glory of God will be revealed in us (Romans 8:18). I'm thankful that despite this journey being hard I have daily been shown such grace.

One last moment before I end this chapter. For years and years, I prayed and begged God to heal my daughter. To "fix" her. To wave His hand and just transform her back into a happy, giggling little girl instead of one who, at almost 20 years old, functions at perhaps a five-year-old level. A few years ago, I had gone grocery shopping; Kaitlyn loved to come out and get the bags of groceries from my car. That was "her" job and she loved it. She came walking down the driveway smiling and swinging her arms. Her face was calm and happy. In that moment, it was like God was whispering to me that she was just who He had made her to be. For the most part, she is content. She has no idea that she is different—she really doesn't. She doesn't feel isolated like the rest of us do—she gets very anxious around a lot of people and new situations, so she feels comfortable in her routine being at school and at home. She does okay at church, and she loves Gatlinburg, so that is our vacation spot. Do I yearn sometimes to try something new? Sure. But her requiring a schedule and consistency has made me require a schedule and consistency—what she needs is now what we all need. Yes, every once in a while, it is stifling. Yes, I gave up my dreams of "normal" motherhood with autism. Yes, I get horribly, terribly lonely—my other girls do too. There are things Kaitlyn will never do—she'll never drive, never be able to live independently; we will never be "empty nesters." But I finally reached a contentment that day that God made Kaitlyn just exactly who He needed and wanted her to be. My role, as best as possible, is to accept that and help her be the best Kaitlyn I can help her be.

Point of reflection: Have you ever entered a "wilderness season"? My pastor recently preached a series of messages on this topic; he referenced back to the Israelites who wandered in the wilderness for 40 years. Their wilderness season was brought on by their own sin and poor decisions. Sometimes, though, we enter "wilderness seasons" that are God allowed and not related to anything we did.

Autism has definitely been my longest and most difficult wilderness season. There I have felt alone, abandoned, and at times just unable to reach God. BUT I have also known times of fellowship with Jesus that I never would have had except for that wilderness. As much as I am loathe to admit it, I never would have sought God so desperately except during those wilderness times when I NEEDED God and He was the only one Who could help...be it through calm, peace, a "small" miracle at the right moment...in a word, GRACE.

Deuteronomy 2:7 says, "For the Lord thy God hath blessed thee in all the works of thy hand: he knoweth thy walking through this great wilderness: these forty years the Lord thy God hath been with thee; thou has lacked nothing." Deuteronomy 8:2: "And thou shalt remember all the way which the Lord thy God led thee these forty years in the wilderness, to humble thee, and to prove thee, to know what was in thine heart, whether thou wouldest keep his commandments, or no." The verses following this outline His promise to the Israelites, that once they were in the promised land (a good land), they would "eat bread without scarceness" (vs 9) but also warned them that if they (the Israelites) forgot Who had brought them through the wilderness, they would be tested again.

In the wilderness, God will prove you; but He will provide for you. He will challenge you to obedience, but His reward is so very great! My challenge? If you are in a wilderness, keep obeying Him. Keep walking the path every day He calls you. I don't know if my wilderness of autism will end or when, but I know with absolute certainty that God in His grace and mercy will still provide and still bless me if I continue to obey Him.

CHAPTER TWELVE

The 40's—
Our Broken Years

THIS BEGINS THE decade that Franky and I gutted our way through. Franky is blissfully 50 now (we celebrated that by going to Dollywood and Splash Country on two consecutive days; I'm still regretting it, but he had a blast!); I'll be 50 this year. Needless to say, I'll be celebrating in slightly more sedate fashion than he did!! You might be thinking—really—you're in your 40's? How bad could it be? Let me tell you our story and then you can decide!

The story begins, really, when I was in nursing school. Fun fact about nurses learning our skills—we like to listen to the body!! Everybody is subject to our practicing! I listened to my heart sounds, my best friend's heart sounds—normal. (I was born with a tiny hole in my heart, but it closed on its own—actually pretty common.) Listened to Franky's; lo and behold I heard a murmur. Quick explanation there: when you hear a murmur, it's a problem with one of the valves in the heart closing incorrectly, so that sound is blood swishing past. This was in 1999; it was a very faint murmur. He did go to the doc and had it checked; he had a very slight issue with his mitral valve. We don't do anything about that until you start having symptoms. Fast forward to 2013—his murmur had been stable for all that time until it wasn't. He started having symptoms—mostly just fatigue—then issues with his heart racing. In December that year he finally fessed up and told me how exhausted he was. Mind you, this was when H1N1 flu was around—I was working A LOT. I mean, A LOT A LOT. We had people on specialized equipment; I was pulling crazy hours. I noticed him sleeping much more and asked if he was okay. We had already done the Holter monitor for the rhythm issues; that didn't reveal anything awful. We both knew it was a matter of when he would have to have his valve worked on.

January 2014 became a whirlwind of activity. Echo, TEE, heart cath all within about a month. I had been talking to my surgeon about Franky—have I mentioned yet how thankful I am that God placed me in my unit working with an amazing surgeon? Well, we were already doing background planning and I knew I would be filing paperwork soon to take a leave of absence to take care of him. Did Franky know this? Well, maybe. Ha!

During this time, because life is just too fun to deal with only one problem at a time, we were having some issues with Kaitlyn's autism. There was also some major planning going on knowing, for the first time since maternity leave, that I would be the stay-at-home parent. Easy peasy, right? Nope!! I was more terrified of that than work! I had classes and more teaching and training to do my job! Parenting? Umm, no. But wait, you say—I'm the mom! I've got this! Oh, sure I did! HA!! Kaitlyn was almost 12, Erica was 10, and Nat was almost five. Thankfully they were all at one school! That's one big moment of grace already!!

Enter. More. Grace. Front and center.

Where to begin? That time period was just wild and overwhelming—and I'm a CVICU nurse! I knew the testing and what was coming up but being thrown into it in my own life—well, let's just say it's a very different experience. We also had a new pastor at our church; I absolutely adore him and his sweet wife! At the time, I didn't know him very well; Franky hardly knew him because he sat with Kaitlyn in children's church. (Before anyone asks, yes, I did ask him if he wanted me to sit with her so he could go to church; the answer was always no. He wanted me to be able to sing in the choir. He knew that was my ministry and he felt his ministry was staying with Kaitlyn.)

What did our pastor do then? He prayed—and let me tell you, this man believes in the power of effectual fervent prayer! He texted. He called.

Those amazing, sweet people that I've gone to church with for years? They enveloped me. They held up my arms like Joshua and Aaron did for Moses; there was simply no way I could do this myself. For two Sundays before Franky's surgery, I basically laid at the altar confessing my fears before God; confessing my lack of faith; fears I would lose my husband before or after the surgery or he would have some complication. By this point, I had worked with postop heart surgery patients for 12 years; sometimes unpredictable things happen in the OR. It wasn't the surgery itself; it was the unknown. And I knew just a leeeeeetle too much for my own good!

God in His abundant mercy absolutely showered us with grace. Franky's valve had just blown open so quickly. In His timing, the first echo got done quickly; I remember telling Franky if we didn't get the postcard reminder in the mail for his echo, I would call that day. Guess what? The postcard for his scheduled echo came that day. We met with his cardiologist a couple weeks later and we got the TEE scheduled (it's a more advanced echo that sizes the valve and looks in more detail at structures) soon afterward. After the TEE was done (and I could hear when the cardiologist turned the sound on—WOW that valve noise was bad!), I met with the doc, and he showed me how bad it was. Then came the heart cath scheduling. His TEE was Thursday. His doc asked who I wanted to do his heart cath—I named my preference; I work with the cardiologists as well. He told me that doc was pretty busy, so I named a couple of others. As I was walking out to my car to pull around and pick up Franky post procedure, I got a phone call from the cardiologist's office—his heart cath would be the coming Monday at 0730. I'm not sure what strings his doc pulled, but I sure was thankful!! Was this a coincidence? Absolutely not. God was already working behind the scenes to set all this up!!

Monday morning, he had his heart cath. His coronary arteries were clear, thankfully—although he does have some unique congenital anomalies! Franky got to meet my surgeon after his cath. So let me tell you a smidge about my heart surgeon. First, he has no idea he is in this book. Second, the man is brilliant. Like, scary brilliant. Instead of building a better mousetrap, he just disassembles the first mousetrap and rebuilds it to his liking. Third, he really truly cares about his patients. Is he a saint? Nope. Do we get along and always have? About 90% of the time actually! He is dedicated beyond belief to what he does!!

More grace—God placed me not only in this line of work, but He placed me, in His wisdom, with just the right surgeon. He also gave me some of the most amazing coworkers ever!! I mean—EVER. I try desperately not to react to things at work. At times with Kaitlyn, I have cried over being so frustrated; when you work in critical care you really have to leave your personal life at the door. The Saturday night before Franky's surgery on Tuesday was my last night at work—I was teary eyed on and off all night. God put me in the room with a good friend; he was so supportive and caring. I'll forever be grateful.

Morning of surgery came; I had fasted and prayed, knowing I was leaving my Hoob in great hands, but I was a ball of nerves. But even in that moment? Grace. How? Now, when I talk to family members, I can look them in the eye and tell them I know exactly what they are going through—those waiting room moments are hard!! It is just our God to turn a moment like this into an opportunity to minister to others!

Another moment? So many, actually.

I was by myself that day. My best friend stayed the night at my house and took the girls to school. We had arranged for people to pick them up; it took some serious coordination to get all this down! That day, I was alone. It was a sinking abyss to be in—I do not recommend! I knew exactly what my husband would be going through in the OR— now, I've never been on bypass, but I know what the surgery involves. I knew what could happen if things went south. I had picked his nurses in my unit to recover him which was a huge blessing. You see, Franky with his Asperger's traits needed certain personalities—really, everyone needs to be matched with the right person! When I'm in charge it's one of the bigger challenges we face! Not everyone will get along equally well; I don't want to make things worse assigning mismatches to patients and nurses!

But still…I was alone. Right? No…I wasn't. Not really.

Those times, when it seems like there is no one there, are the times when you can really, REALLY feel the near tangible presence of the One Who made Franky right there; the very One you need to comfort you, reassure you, and give you peace that passes all understanding.

And He was there—and suddenly I wasn't alone.

I was in the waiting room, crocheting furiously and praying (I crocheted a lot during that day; the tendency is the more anxious I get the faster I crochet—it was almost impressive that day!!). I had a plan—once he was on bypass, I would get coffee and something to eat. It took almost two hours for the call that he was on bypass; it takes more prep time for the approach they took for his surgery. Once I got that phone call from the OR—oh my word the total indescribable peace. Whew. I knew beyond a shadow of a doubt he would be ok, and I had absolutely no control anymore. Isn't that funny? You would think I would have LESS peace then!! But really—what could I do now? Pray. That's it!! And I knew many, many others were praying as well—so I just let go and let God!

I schlepped downstairs to get coffee and a bagel. When I got downstairs, I ran into one of the vascular fellows I was friends with. He asked why I was there in regular clothes (we don't know each other out of scrubs!!). Long story short—he bought my breakfast!! Went to get coffee at Starbucks—one of the perfusionists just "happened" to be there—he bought my coffee!! I know I've said this before, but there are no "just so happened" moments—God had timed this out as well!! (By the way, perfusionists run the bypass machines, in case anyone was wondering.)

Another huge moment of grace? I was able to sneak back into the unit and wait in there while Franky was in the OR. I hung with my work buddies while I waited. In truth—I wasn't alone anymore! As soon as Franky rolled out of surgery, I got to see him. Honestly, I think my coworkers thought I would freak out when I saw him but I'm just not that way.

Grace, my friends, is in those small moments.

Grace is God sneaking you an itty bitty blessing and letting you recognize it for that.

(These are my personal ideas—just what I've seen in my own life!)

Grace is feeling so stressed about something, desperately trying to pray and give it over to God and feeling the veil of sweet peace cover you.

Franky ended up spending 12 days in the hospital. 12 long days. He had some small complications—well, I consider them small—two CT scans, multiple X rays, and an extra drainage tube, but hey! They thought he might need a pacemaker after surgery—but God took care of that! He very well could have gotten a postop infection—nope! He came home with a very small drainage tube—that stayed in for four days before I took him back in and he was able to get it removed. Boy howdy, did I ever learn to respect his job as a stay-at-home dad!! Juggling schedules, keeping up with dishes, laundry, etc, with young kids who were struggling with dad not being there!! More grace? The day we picked up Franky from the hospital, later on, the girls started getting sick—they had picked up a GI bug, but praise God Franky didn't get it!! I cannot imagine how much worse he would have felt if he had started puking!

Even more grace—we have always struggled with trying to find help with the girls for babysitting, etc. That first week, we had help every day! I was so grateful!! When I say this, I am not saying that no one cares—everyone is just busy, and we don't have lots of family here. Life is busy! It just is what it is! With my whacked out third shift schedule, our life seems a little insane sometimes. I will say, my husband has so much respect for my surgeon now; and it has cemented a strong professional relationship into some degree of friendship. Other friendships with nurses, respiratory therapists, and perfusionists were strengthened with this experience as well! One other moment of grace: until you are in this place, it is almost impossible to comprehend how much you lose control of your whole schedule to the medical world. Now I strive to be much more compassionate to family members trying to coordinate phone calls and visits—life just doesn't stop! Six weeks after Franky's surgery, we were able to take a well-deserved few days in the mountains—praise God, he was healed enough to make the trip and just enjoy quiet moments on the porch of the property we rented. We definitely grew closer as a couple during that time.

Well, now Franky is fixed—and then I started breaking down…

I will say, Franky's breaking and fixing was more dramatic; that's saying something for someone who just does not embody drama. I don't mean that in a bad way—this is the man who was dealing with one of Kaitlyn's meltdowns one day and calmly looked at me and said, "The fire's flaming"—and went right back outside to grilling hamburgers. Didn't. Bat. An. Eyelash. My breaking was more like an old car breaking down and needing replacement parts—at least that's what it felt like. Sometimes I couldn't find parts in time. Ha!!

How do I sum up, personally, the years of 41 through 49 for me?

It started innocently for me; my right knee started hurting in June of 2014. I knew this one would be my "problem child." I had had a pretty bad but poorly treated ice-skating injury when I was a senior in college. I landed with all my weight on my bent right knee, and I discovered to my dismay as I struggled not to pass out from the pain (lying flat on my back on the ice) that you truly do see stars. Pretty, twinkling stars. This coming from the chick who had all four wisdom teeth removed with just local injections—I refused to let them put me to sleep. The good thing about the wisdom teeth? God showed me just how poorly I tolerate pain meds—this would be a strange blessing 25 years later! But I digress.

So…I met my first ortho surgeon in June 2014. Notice how I said my first one? Hold onto your hats, folks…

First steroid injection in said knee June 2014. I had a weird reaction to it—they called it a flare reaction, which in retrospect it wasn't, but it took me a while to learn. Physical therapy—round one.

October 1, 2014. I woke up that day with "my neck is killing me." Now prior to this, I had had little twinges in that shoulder—nothing to slow me down. I had played so many sports in high school and college that "twinges" were nothing. I waited a week and went to the doc. I couldn't sleep for the pain. PT rounds two, three, and four. MRI number two. (The first was my right knee.) Second steroid injection attempt—I say attempt because the reaction was so bad, I was advised to call in to work and take a hefty dose of Benadryl. Also found out I am WAY sensitive to adhesives and cannot use kinesiology tape (they use it to help stabilize joints and muscles). Add to allergy list number whatever—I am, indeed, fearfully and wonderfully made!!

January 2015. Met my second ortho surgeon. Wait, I'm not done! There are more…anyhoo, this one said the magic words—sweetheart, I can help you! Yes—he said exactly that! He injected my shoulder with lidocaine to figure out where the worst of the pain was, and I nearly cried with relief after three and a half months of unending neck and shoulder pain!

March 2015. First ortho surgery—labrum tear left shoulder; cut my biceps tendon and reimplanted it in my humerus along with cleaning out arthritis at the end of my collarbone that had basically had my joint "stuck" for six months. Wanna talk about bruising? Whew. Fifth round of PT.

Narcotics. Nerve/muscle stimulators. Splints. On Q pain balls filled with numbing agents to help with pain. Dry heaving after surgery. Ice machines.

Lather, rinse, repeat.

PT, X rays, MRI's. Patch me up and put me back in the game, coach—I'm good.

Shots. Steroid injections, hyaluronic acid injections, splints to every moveable part it seemed. Well, not my ankles. Thank you, Jesus, for small mercies!! I think I'm up to 25 or 30 steroid injections and 28 injections to replace normal joint fluid—plus two times having fluid drawn off my left knee. 14 MRI's? 17? I'm not sure. Lost count on X rays as well.

Recovery postop. Regain strength. Get moving again. Pain free for a while—never knowing after a while when the next round would hit and trying to live in the moments in between. "Thank You, Jesus, for Your mercy" moments in between the pain.

Periods of wracking pain. Every step hurt; every movement hurt. Deep breathing exercises. Questioning my sanity. Begging God to "fix" me. Begging Him for relief. Asking Him why. Confessing to sins I wasn't sure I had committed but figured I should cover the bases just in case; then confessed again to what I had already dealt with. Ha! In truth, there were days and nights where I honestly didn't think I would make it one. More. Day. And I didn't want to, to tell the truth. I would pray for God to just take me home. The only thing I could keep telling myself was He still had something He wanted me to do; I would think of my girls and fight my mind for them. At those times, there just wasn't anything I felt like hanging around this pretty blue planet for…every day was misery. Was I depressed? Maybe (probably)—would I go to the doc for that or admit it? Hard no. Big fat no. Looking back, I wish I had; I wish I had gotten some help. Thank God, He sustained me.

Lack of sleep. Can't sleep without pain pills, muscle relaxants, Benadryl, melatonin. Can't sleep in my bed—that was a really bad spell. For a year, because of my hip and back, after work, I slept in my recliner.

Then bought another recliner. You can only imagine the strain it put on every single relationship—my husband, my kids who had to tiptoe around me (literally, because I had to sleep in the living room!), my poor coworkers—did I mention in between surgeries I was still working around 48 hours a week and rarely called in? Yeah. Was I nice? Ummmm....

So...here's what I've had done.

Left shoulder surgery. Right knee surgery. Right elbow surgery (compensatory injury from the left shoulder going bad)—that was rough! Resected my common extensor tendon (think tennis elbow) and reimplanted it in my radius. Left hip surgery (labrum tear—that was fun! I hate crutches!); repeat right knee surgery four weeks later. Left hip replacement—this is when I met my third and fourth ortho surgeons trying to figure out a plan of care/action for me. (Because, really—shouldn't everyone have weird complications? Just me? Yes?) Left knee surgery. Right shoulder surgery (about the same as the left shoulder). Right carpal tunnel release. Spinal cord stimulator placement—the permanent one—after the trial lead was done and a bunch of injections and failed attempts to temporarily "fry" the nerves in my back. (I've got three discs in various degrees of disrepair in my back, and I have arthritis all through my lower spine, in case you were wondering.) Redo left knee surgery. Whew. And upcoming? My left knee is bum—again—and my right knee is on borrowed time, so it'll be a double knee replacement for 1000, Alex!!! (As I type this, I have an appointment in a couple of days to see my surgeon AGAIN—hopefully to pull some fluid off and then try the hyaluronic acid injection to properly cushion this bad boy.)

I'm going to indulge myself here—I keep telling a friend of mine that this chapter was hard to write, then the next chapter, and the next—and it's true. Every single chapter in this book has, in its own way, been hard to write. I am forcing myself down some very difficult memory lanes in some of these; at least with a few I can say they are well and truly in the past and they ain't coming back. This chapter? Well...when will the end be? I don't know. I joke that maybe, once my knees are replaced,

I'll be bionic and all good then—and I'll feel a twinge in my right hip and cringe internally before I move on.

I've got another dear friend who tells of his own story with sickness that I'm going to borrow a paraphrased quote from. His wife, a dear lovely friend, was having health issues. He felt terrible about it and wanted to "fix" things for her. Then his son was having some issues that turned out to not be as severe as thought, praise God. Again, he felt terrible and wanted to "fix" things. Then his own health issues started. As bad as he felt wanting his wife and son to be whole and healthy, when you start feeling sick/broken/in pain, it's different—you can't escape it. That's where I am. I haven't been able to escape my own body for the past eight years; you're on an emotional tightrope.

This body of mine that was so strong for so many years…that allowed me to work seemingly ridiculous hours, some while pregnant, and just keep plugging forward, has failed to a degree. Yes, I can work now, and I am working. But it's the "extra" stuff. Here's my self-indulgent moment number one: I used to LOVE to wear high heels. Shocked? I'm 5'10"—who needs heels? Honestly, I loved them because I loved how they made me look and feel. I felt pretty. It was fun. It was different than wearing scrubs four and five nights a week with work clogs and being all business. For church, once a week, I would put on some serious, ridiculous, five-inch heels…I loved it. Guess what? When your knees, hip, and back are jacked the heels gotta go. I can wear some "low" heels now, every once in a while, and I'm thankful, don't get me wrong. But I boxed up a serious collection of fancy heels and cried my eyes out doing it after my first hip surgery. I felt like I was putting away "childish things." My husband didn't get it—not one little bit. Those heels were part of my identity though; and when your identity is tied up 99% of the time in being an autism mom and a critical care nurse working like I did, that itty bitty part that felt "mine" and was pretty heartbreaking.

The other part I have had to let go of in these past few years was my athletic self, my graceful self. I told a physical therapist after my hip replacement I had to "box up" my athlete and put her away on a shelf. She laughed at me. (P.S.—that did not make me happy, just sayin'.) She then suggested maybe I should just try yoga—after many PT's have told me absolutely NO yoga because that's part of my joint issues; I'm overly flexible and it's allowed my lax joints to wear down much faster. Another PT heard the exchange and said, "Mel, I'm sorry—that's hard losing a part of yourself." Needless to say, this one got it. Over the years I've lost chunks of "myself." I'm not saying they were good chunks, but the athletic part especially fed that part of me that was so self-sufficient and strong. Man, do I hate needing help and feeling weak, especially after learning to "handle" life by myself from an early age. OK, pity party over—moving on to lessons learned!

So where, in the middle of all this, is grace?

Grace is God leading me to some amazing surgeons. Grace is God making me strong enough, one day at a time, to deal with this. Grace is a quiet, stoic husband who listened to me sob on the way home from work telling him I can't do this anymore—and then making me coffee when I woke up so I can go back in to work.

Grace is even in the complications…the times when the surgeon has come out and said it was worse than what we thought…the imaging didn't show that…that's still grace. How? Well, now when I call or message them and tell them something's off…they listen. They know me now. They know my pain tolerance, and they know I wait at least a week or two until I know something is wrong. And it'll probably serve me again soon…my ortho told me flat out my imaging just never seems right; things won't look that bad, then when they get in there it's worse—so now with needing my knee replaced soon that will work (in the weirdest way possible) in my favor.

Another complication that possibly saved my life? Blood clots. But wait…oh yes. After my first knee surgery, three and a half weeks later (which is weird in its own right) I developed clots in my leg. (I also had issues with the blood vessels in my legs—specifically my right leg—that prompted me to have something called sclerotherapy to fix the veins—LOTS of needles there!) Enter the blood thinners. Enter my weird reaction to meds. Enter ultrasounds, losing A LOT of blood when I had my period (sorry guys, it's my book!)…but here's the weird thing. When I went back to the vascular docs about it after pushing to get my blood levels checked and realizing I had lost three grams of hemoglobin, the vascular doc looked at me and apologized. But for what? This med was newer…they didn't realize how potent it would be to women still getting their periods. She told me other patients had started calling, but I called first. That was a HUGE moment of grace, me and my big mouth! Also, though, now I have to take meds to prevent blood clots after every lower body surgery to keep more from forming. Since I'm allergic to aspirin, it has to be one of the newer ones. Those clots also have me wearing compression hose at work—I sure wouldn't wear them otherwise!! (They're really uncomfortable!!) But the holy God of heaven protected me time and again in that. Did He maybe use my little incident then to help protect other women? Maybe so—and if He did, to Him be the glory!! There is much grace in God's protection!

There is grace even in my weird reactions to meds…I always reacted to the steroid injections I got for my joints, but as time has gone on those reactions have gotten worse, to the point where I cannot take steroids anymore, and it took an allergist to figure out what was going on. How is there grace there? Well, that reaction I have, if I continued to get the injections, could have gotten really bad—so the grace there is God giving me that nudge that something was wrong and causing me to start researching, and also who to call and ask about the reaction! His divine protection—yet again!!

Grace is crying out to God and asking if it's ok for me to take pain pills (remember my mom??) and getting a feeling of peace. Grace is God knowing that I would need time off to deal with deaths in the family—and four times that happened I was recovering from surgery. Four. Times. My brother-in-law (shot himself in the head while drunk), my father-in-law, my dad (complications from a massive stroke), and one of my best friends (cardiac arrest).

Now, how on earth is there grace in dealing with death? Seriously Mel—what is WRONG with you??

But how is there NOT grace?

God knew when these precious souls were leaving this earth—and He knew that I would have to have time to process. And plan. Somehow, I ended up planning a lot of things dealing with these—whoa. And He knew I would keep trying to plug along and work and never give myself time to process, grieve—I'm bad about that. Box it up and keep going. Sometimes you just have to do that; eventually you'll have to deal though. I'm grateful God more or less forced me to deal right then and not drag it back out of that painful box.

There really has been so much grace through this hard, painful eight years—so much it would be a whole book to list every example. Because it's not like you're not dealing with everything else too…autism never stops, in case you were wondering! And bills still have to get paid…and they all got paid. We never missed a bill!

Grace through friends praying. Gift cards and a little extra money sent our way just when we needed it. Grace that insurance covered all but what we could afford—that ain't just a coincidence, folks. Grace when I felt suffocated in my spirit and someone saying just what I needed to lift my load. Grace through messages at church—sermons that chastised me, challenged me, broke me a little, encouraged me—but upheld me. All of these are of God's grace. Grace through music—hearing just the right song at the right time on the radio.

Grace is God caring enough about me to not let me stay where I was/ am—grace is God refining me; filing down and shaving away at my rough areas and causing me to grow. Philippians 1:6 says, "Being confident of this very thing, that he which hath begun a good work in you will perform it until the day of Jesus Christ:"—I promise you, folks, that good work that began in me when I got saved was not at all complete that day. I've got many things that God is still trying to refine in me; some days I desperately wish my lessons and growing were done but I know that the day He deems me complete I will be in heaven; so I carry on and try my best in His strength to do what He wants me to do and be who He wants me to be.

Grace is God teaching me to rely on Him. Fully and completely. Grace is God causing me to seek Him more, both in prayer and reading His word.

Grace is God causing me to rely on His strength and not mine.

Grace is God allowing me to "suffer a little while" so at times I would truly appreciate when things were better; sometimes you truly don't appreciate the gifts God has given you until things are temporarily removed.

Grace is God giving you a verse to cling to...many days and nights it was Galations 6:9: "And let us not be weary in well doing: for in due season we shall reap, if we faint not." There were times I sure didn't feel like I was "well doing" much of anything, but I assure you I tried. There were also times I asked God when my "due season" was (I still do ask that, in case you're wondering...), and by the way, what exactly am I reaping? OK, I'm not the best Christian from time to time and I'll own it...but I learned to desperately cling to that promise that one day, it'll be worth it all...it might not be here, it might be in heaven, but one day...when I see Jesus face to face. It's hard sometimes, this Christian walk—it's freeing once you learn to trust and your faith grows, but in the interim when you're looking down a path that seems endless, faith is honestly just being determined to believe what's in the Bible—gritting your teeth and telling God I trust You no matter what...but you have to *choose* to do that every. Single. Day.

Every day pain free is a gift from God.

Every day with pain is a day to remember that it won't always be this bad and to lean in on Jesus and rest on His promises—some days literally claiming by faith alone, desperately, that the same God who gave Paul and Silas songs to sing in prison shackled to a wall will be the same God who will give me songs and comfort me. Grace is God letting me meet one of my favorite gospel singers and buy a bunch of his music three months before my hip replacement. Did I "need" that music? Could I have survived without it? I'm sure. Did God bless me mightily allowing me to have that music to help calm and soothe me? So much so!!

Every day is a day to be thankful for everything God has given me, whether good or bad. Sometimes the bad I've experienced is merely a way I can minister to someone else—I've learned this many times over.

Grace is in the process.

Grace is in the pain. You can't know relief without the pain. And you can't know the fellowship of His suffering without…suffering. (Philippians 3:10)

Grace is in the learning. Holy cow, what I have learned about myself; what I've learned about compassion and kindness; what I've learned about empathy; what I've learned about extending grace to others. How many times I've had to look inward and ask forgiveness for weakness and failures; how many times I've had to come to a point of brokenness and realize that not only do I not have to do for myself, but I CANNOT. And OH the freedom in that little phrase!!

My favorite verse for this whole time period? Romans 12:15—"Rejoice with them that do rejoice, and weep with them that do weep." Why this verse? Because honestly—these past few years, I have experienced suffering like I never had before. I have dealt with mental pain, emotional pain, psychological pain—but whatever I was going through prior to this, as hard as autism was or work was or dealing with the loss of my mom or whatever it was—I would say, thank you God I've got my job and for making me strong. Thank You that I can work out and have a way to exorcise some of this negative energy.

Up until this decade, I was still relying more on two things than God to sustain me—my work and my physical body. It wasn't what I looked like. Honestly and truly, it was not. It was the fact that I'm sort of like a Timex—take a licking and keep on ticking. Up until this point I had such a stupid high pain tolerance (I still have that high pain tolerance but let me tell you—it is wearying after a while!) and the ability to "shake it off." These past eight years I have hit wall after wall; time after time of being "shut down" physically—and I've been forced many times to rely only on the One who made me. I can't think to myself anymore that at least I'm still strong—because no matter what people think of me, the strength they see is only from God. It's gotten to the point where I am almost jumpy when I start having consistent pain—what's broken now?? I can't trust my body anymore. God knows my weaknesses as well as my strengths; it is He who gives me strength and not this frail body!

That verse about weep with those who weep?

I'm not naturally compassionate. And yes…oops…I'm a nurse… I'm a hard nose by nature. I am. I've allowed life to make me hard. For years I thought the hardness was toughness; now I know it isn't. The hardness was (and is sometimes) bitterness; it's still something I struggle with. I'll say again—when it's your body and you can't escape it, it's different. Daily chronic pain changes you. You can't escape from it. It has forced me to turn to Jesus and not rely on me—but it has also softened me. It has given me sympathy and empathy I never thought I could have; it has made me a better nurse. It has made me a more compassionate person.

I can really teach my patients pain control techniques that have helped me. My patients that dry heave after surgery? Definitely have sympathy there! The patients who need to move half an inch? Yeah, I get that now. Can't sleep in the bed because they can't get comfortable? I hear you!! I spent a year in my recliner before God provided the opportunity, the timing, and the finances for my fancy expensive bed. Boy, talk about grace!!! Sure, I'll give pain meds to my patients—but now I know propping someone's arm or leg just a little differently or shifting a pillow an inch is sometimes more important! Do I get annoyed sometimes? Sure. I also get hideously annoyed with myself too!

Don't get me wrong. I am so stupid sick of this frail skeleton I have. When you are forced to go from being strong and athletic to not being able to do anything except work it is awful! Yes—I enjoy my job. I would love to do something besides my job some days though. When your whole mindset has to change and now you have to be careful walking, your mindset changes. Is it worth taking that walk, especially if I have to go to work later? Those are the decisions I weigh on the daily! I don't trust my body the way I used to. I need to rest more. I need downtime more. And sometimes I get "forced" into "timeout" (my phrase); there the Lord slows me way, way down! Not only has He gotten my attention in relying solely on Him, He has also made me swallow my pride and ask for help!

You see, pride and bitterness for me go hand in hand. I hate that I see this about me now, and that it took so much for me to see it at all! Man, do I wish I hadn't had to learn this lesson!! But oh, the grace in the learning! When you've had to raise yourself emotionally and you feel like you've done ok, it sure gives you a sense of pride. It also gives a sense of hyper independence. Asking for help is HARD because you never needed it before; I learned I couldn't rely on anyone else. Now? My hope is in Jesus! My help is in Jesus…alone!! He has covered me in grace and taught me that He puts people in my life for a reason. He has given me a trust in Him I never had before; He has also caused me to become softer to other people, both in giving and receiving.

To end this chapter, yes—it HAS been hard. Yes, I would love if I hadn't had to go through 11 surgeries, MRI's, rounds of PT, countless injections—but I wouldn't trade any of it for what God has taught me and the grace He has given me. I am different than I was at near 50 than I was at 40. I'm not nearly as toned and tight physically—I'm a little fluffy, and I'm trying hard to be OK with that! But I'm so much nicer, kinder, and more forgiving of myself and others. I'm more willing to give and receive grace. I am a testament to the grace of almighty God. He is still working on me every day!!

Point of reflection: Have you ever experienced physical pain to the point where your entire life was affected? If you haven't, I am so very thankful for you—and I won't wish it on you for anything. In. The. World. That being said...for those of you reading this who have dealt with severe pain or chronic pain—you know that there isn't an area it doesn't touch.

What to do during that time? What can you remember about our Savior, where can you turn to in the Bible for strength and comfort? First, remember that this suffering is temporary—even if it lasts the rest of our lives, in Heaven there is no more suffering. Romans 8:18 states "For I reckon that the sufferings of this present time are not worthy to be compared with the glory which shall be revealed in us." These words are attributed to apostle Paul—remember the man who suffered shipwrecks, multiple beatings and stoning, being whipped, imprisoned, and who knows what else—and by golly, if he was able to pen them with this confidence, I am going to claim them as well! Do I know when my suffering will end? Nope. But will it be worth it for the glory revealed in us? YES.

Second, that suffering has a purpose; we might not be able to figure out WHY or WHEN but take comfort in I Peter 5:10: "But the God of all grace, who hath called us unto his eternal glory by Christ Jesus, after that ye have suffered a while, make you perfect, stablish, strengthen, settle you." Perfect here does not mean sinless; it means complete. Stablish, strengthen, settle—these words make me think of a home with a solid foundation that will not be jarred in a storm. Will winds shake the walls and windows at times? Yes. Maybe even break those windows or tear off shingles from the roof. Will the home stand? Again—YES. That's what Jesus is accomplishing through this, friends...our foundation becomes more secure when we walk through those moments WITH God and even in the hard times, choose to trust!

Third, remember Who suffered all things while on earth—praise God, we have a Savior Who has experienced all that we will! He was despised, rejected, reviled, cursed—over and over. He experienced physical pain that I cannot even comprehend and makes me cry just to think about. Our Savior went to Calvary, was beaten, had a crown of thorns jammed onto His head, and hung on a cross for hours to redeem our souls—He gave His life for mine and yours! "For we have not an high priest which cannot be touched with the feeling of our infirmities; but was in all points tempted like as we are, yet without sin." (Hebrews 4:15). He was tempted for us, He suffered for us, and He lives for us!

CHAPTER THIRTEEN

The Grace of Loss

WELL, WHAT A title for this chapter. Initially I had it titled the pain of loss, and that is true—loss can be painful, any loss, at least initially. Even years later, loss can hurt; it takes time to realize there can indeed be grace found in loss.

I have some dear friends who have recently lost parents; my heart hurts for them. There is no right or wrong in the grieving process—my personal opinion. There are nursing and psych theories to go along with the grieving process; I won't include those, don't worry; but the grieving process can be messy and heartrending. You also can't put a time limit on that process; you might think, oh, I'm doing ok today then a random memory of your loved one will just flat smack you between the eyes for a minute. What I can absolutely and completely promise is that the same God Who saved me can heal your heart as you grieve; He will give you the grace to sustain you!

I have lost both of my parents. My mom's death I already dealt with in detail in an earlier chapter. The only thing I will reiterate with that is the grace that sustained me during that time also sustained me later;

each loss was different though. The next loss after my mom's passing was my brother-in-law, Chanse. I mentioned earlier that he died after my first knee surgery. Can I just say, the Lord's timing is definitely not mine? Two days after my knee surgery, my phone started ringing; it was a local number but not one I knew. Why is this important? Because I, like most other people, don't answer the phone when we don't know the number—but God prompted me to answer this call!!

It turned out to be the hospital that I work at. The patient liaison was calling on behalf of my in-laws wanting to speak to me. Side note: when you get that type of call, it's almost never good news. Trust me. I started the conversation with yes, that is my brother-in-law—while looking at my husband and mouthing "It's Chanse". Grief floated over his face. You see, Chanse had battled alcoholism for years; he never made good decisions drunk—argue with me if you want, it's just not possible to make good decisions while drunk! This time, the decision was permanent. He had been drinking and arguing with his girlfriend. He turned to her and said, "Watch this"—and put a loaded gun to his head and pulled the trigger.

Chanse wasn't legally brain dead though. Sadly, he had one or two reflexes that kept him on a vent and other machines and meds for a week. My in laws had made peace and were asking to please just let him go; legally the hospital couldn't. You see, my in laws made the amazing decision to donate Chanse's organs to help someone else. I'm always in awe of this selfless decision! Unfortunately, with all of the protocols in place, they have to make sure everything is done correctly before they take someone off the ventilator to do organ donation—I get that side. It's just a very difficult place to be in limbo with. With all these terrible circumstances though, where in the world can I possibly find grace?

First, in God's timing. These next couple of sentences might seem really self-centered, but they are not meant to be, so I'll just dive in here. It was two days after my first knee surgery. I was literally immobile—I couldn't drive, had a hard time walking, BUT I could stay with the girls. It was also summer break. Horrible times, awful heartbreak—but God allowed this to happen in a time that I was already off work and could allow my husband all the time he needed to help his family. Second, He gave extra grace in his being at my hospital—even to knowing his nurses well and having peace that he was well and compassionately cared for. I can almost hear the questions—but if he was already mostly gone, his brain destroyed by that bullet, why would this matter? For nurses, we still care not only for that patient—no matter how bad they are, no matter what the circumstances are, until their soul leaves their body they are a PERSON. Also, we care for their family. In circumstances like these, that becomes a huge priority—you have a family that has made a tremendously selfless decision and it is HARD. The emotional toll is high. Our job is to support them, hold hands, let them cry on us…and those nurses did that work so very, very well.

The third moment—my other brother-in-law Chris was able to make it home. You see, at the time, he was hiking the Appalachian Trail—it's the hiking trail through the Appalachian Mountains going from Georgia all the way up to Maine. Communication along there is spotty at best; cell phone reception isn't always available, and you literally never know exactly where someone is on the trail. They were able to reach him and get him back to South Carolina very quickly; his old boss went and picked him up. I'm so thankful he was able to make it back to be able to make peace with everything. Chris was also able to reassure his family that he had talked to Chanse at length about his salvation; they had hiked that trail a couple of years before and had unlimited time to talk.

The fourth and last moment of grace here (there were countless tiny moments; I'm focusing on the "big" ones) was the organ donation group working with his family. I was able to get up to the hospital a couple more times to help with some of the medical jargon (and wow is the jargon a lot at that time!); I ended up becoming friends with one or two of the people working with them. Truthfully, these folks have a very difficult but crucial job and they do it so very well; they ensure patients and families are emotionally supported and they treat people with such dignity. Every once in a while, at work I would see our family's main coordinator after I came back from surgery; he was always so kind and gave me big hugs and "thank you's." I have a much different level of respect seeing these folks now and experiencing their job from both sides. It's another experience where God has given me so much more sympathy and empathy in helping other families. It's still hard; when families cry, I cry; but being able to look someone in the eye and tell them I understand, and mean it? As hard as the whole ordeal was, it's such a comfort to these folks to be able to offer that. There is a different level of understanding, a different level of compassion when you are on a path with someone you've already walked.

I wish I could say Chanse's death was the only one of 2016 that was very close in my family; the next was unexpected as well. Not long before Chanse's death, my dad celebrated his 80th birthday. I made a surprise trip to Pennsylvania to see him. During my visit, he told me he was glad I had come because he wouldn't have another birthday. Now, I don't think this was a doom and gloom moment—he tended to be a negative person, but he was excellent at hiding how bad he felt. I truly believe he knew he was sicker than he let on. From after his birthday until November that year, he had a few falls, a few trips to the hospital, and a lot of other things along the way. Four days after I had elbow surgery to repair a torn tendon (this was a compensatory injury due to overuse of my right arm when my left shoulder was bad) I got a call from my stepmom and then my brother—my dad had had a major stroke and was airlifted to a hospital in Philadelphia (they were about 45 minutes away). On November 30th, eleven days after my surgery, he passed away...peacefully, in hospice... due to complications from his stroke.

Grace, in this situation, again came in the form of timing—up until he passed away, I spent hours of time on the phone with the hospital and family members. God also gave me the knowledge and wisdom to not only understand what was going on, but He also gave me the peace and presence of mind to not only ask before if he would want very aggressive measures taken, but also to be able to explain that to my family. If I had been at work, it would have been incredibly difficult to make even a quarter of those phone calls; also, let me tell you—the stress from dealing with hard situations at home while you're a nurse at the bedside? Whew. God also allowed things to happen at a time when I honestly couldn't do much else but sit and read—my right arm was in a splint and a sling. I wasn't allowed to do so much as wiggle my fingers for the first week after surgery!

But God—the day I was talking with the docs about moving my dad to hospice was the day I had my postop visit with my surgeon; I knew him well enough to look him in the eye and ask, can I drive up to Pennsylvania? I literally hung up the phone with the doc in Philly as I was walking into my appointment with him. Flying wasn't an option due to the amount of equipment I needed to take with me. He cleared me to drive that day in limited amounts, with my reassuring him that I would be mostly on the highway with only a little shifting involved (of course, I drive a stick shift—of course!!!). If he had had that massive stroke a couple of days earlier, I wouldn't have been cleared. Praise God for His impeccable timing!

Another moment of grace? This is going to seem SO dumb, but I remember it so clearly—I took my portable CD player with me. I'll refresh your memory—gospel music has brought me such peace! It sustained me on the drive after my mom passed away. In the car I have now, it doesn't have a CD player and I didn't have any thumb drives (I've solved that problem since then!). My portable CD player hadn't been working at home, but I decided to take it anyway—and it worked!! The God of grace gave me comfort via music on the way up!

I have to add two moments of grace here I almost forgot—first, my brother got to travel to Philadelphia to the hospital there several times. He was able to talk to my dad and communicate to some degree—the stroke left my dad with only the ability to grunt. My brother told me he asked him if he knew he was saved and going to heaven; the best my brother could tell, my dad indicated he was saved. My brother was able to pray with him several times in the hospital. This was important to me; he told us he got saved when I was 12, but my mom insisted he wasn't. Sounds awful, right? I'll just say this—it was a convoluted moment. The other moment was during my dad's memorial service—one of the members of my old church in PA stood up and gave testimony how he had talked with my dad several times when my dad was cleaning the heater at the church. He was able to give additional reassurance that he felt my dad was in heaven. What peace of mind!!

Another moment—my small church I grew up in once more went far above and beyond to be so kind and hospitable to our family. Without hesitation, they opened the doors of the church, left the doors open at odd hours for our family to prepare, and showed such respect in the circumstances. They provided refreshments and even took up an offering for our family. Folks, when you've just had surgery and things come up, you just have to leave it in the hands of our heavenly Father that He will provide for you!! Such grace that even in those moments He did provide!! I also got to talk with my dad's coworker for quite a while at the memorial; I don't know if you recall, but I wasn't close to my dad—partially because I wasn't "allowed" as a child, but truthfully my dad was not easy to get close to. Being able to talk to his coworker and seeing him through his eyes gave me a great measure of peace. God truly is in all the details! His grace extends to all areas!

The last moment of grace I'll recount—I'm leaving several out due to respecting privacy—is how my dad passed. My mom did not pass peacefully. My dad, however, passed away a few minutes after my brother and nephew went to see him one last time. He died peacefully and, I believe, how he wanted to—alone, with no one seeing that last moment of what he would have considered "weakness." I wish I would have been able to see him one last time; I am so thankful Jesus drew him to heaven peacefully.

The third person that passed in such a short span that was so close to our family was my father-in-law. He passed around 14 months after my dad passed away, which would have made it early 2018. He had been getting progressively sicker during the preceding months; he was a diabetic and his kidneys were starting to fail, leading to several hospital visits. The last time he was put in the hospital was about a week after my first hip surgery. Now, I can only imagine what you're beginning to think here—it had gotten to be downright weird that people kept getting sick and then dying around the time I had surgery…and I can't disagree!! The only thing I can keep coming back to is God allowing these at a time when I would have more time and more emotional freedom to deal with the loss, as well as allow my husband extra time at home. I could be totally wrong there though!

My mother-in-law really struggled with my father in law's decline— she had a hard time keeping everything straight and she really leaned on my husband and me. Thankfully, by His grace, with my being off work while he was in the hospital my husband was able to spend more time with him and help his mom. I was on crutches for a couple of weeks, which was *awful,* and I do not recommend—but after that, aside from physical therapy, I was able to spend some precious time with family. With my work schedule, I haven't always had much family time; I am so thankful I had that time!

Another moment of grace? The hospice house he was transferred to was close to our house. The next moment came in my knowing the former director of nursing there—the staff there was already wonderful, but I felt like we did have some "special" treatment having a friend there! I was able to drive by the time he was moved to hospice, which was another moment of grace; I was able to drive over to the hospice house and meet the ambulance there and have a long conversation with the nursing staff on his arrival.

The last big moment of grace involves some scheduling—my life is strange, folks, and I'll be free with that statement! I was scheduled for another surgery the Friday that my father-in-law was transferred to hospice (yes, four weeks after my hip surgery…). My surgeon's office called Thursday and apologized profusely but he was overbooked—could I reschedule my surgery for Monday? Can I just stop here and praise God for His timing? Folks, nothing happens to us that He does not already know about! Take comfort in that!! My father-in-law did not have long on this earth; we didn't know just how short his time was. I rescheduled my surgery for Monday morning. I went to see him Thursday and it hurt to see him suffering. Friday evening my husband went to see his dad. He spent an hour or so there and said his goodbyes. He told me when he got back home that he was surprised he was still alive when he left.

Friday night into Saturday morning, I prayed earnestly that God would have mercy on him, and his suffering would be short. Not ten minutes after I said amen, I got a call from the hospice house that he had passed—and as it turns out, he passed the same minute that I ended my prayer. Friends, I could not even imagine how it would have been if I'd had surgery Friday. My husband would have felt obligated to stay with me and he wouldn't have had that last time with his dad. It was a hard and trying time, but my God of grace and mercy came through as only He could!!

The last loss in this section is particularly hard for me. You know, you cannot change your family—it is who God chooses you to be born into. My pastor preached about a term called oikos—it is your circle of influence. Friends, family, coworkers—whoever is in your "circle." I have been very blessed with my crazy life to have some amazing friends, and Katie influenced me in powerful ways.

Katie was one of those friends who, once she was in your circle, made you realize you couldn't imagine life without her. God brought her to my friend Kristen's life first; Kristen was her nursing instructor. She came into my life because she needed help with chemistry, so Kristen sent her to me. Our bond was instant. We had shared some similar struggles and we shared those with each other very quickly. God gave me her as "my person" through several surgeries, and I was with her for some of hers.

Katie just had a way of blowing into your life with gale force winds despite her small size. You couldn't not love her. She made me laugh till I cried more times than I could count. We would talk for hours and text longer. She taught me how to live life with all I had. I tend to be a cautious person; her all too brief time in my life taught me two things—take the trip and take the picture. My biggest regret with Katie? That I didn't have enough time with her. She loved and lived so much in her 26 ½ years on earth—she just packed it in! My memories of Katie could fill its own book! What I want to focus on is how God gave me grace through her life.

First, the grace of forgiveness. I thought I had an OK handle on that, but she had such a pure and sweet heart, and she embodied forgiveness and letting bitterness go. Second, the grace of learning to really open my heart. You see, I have terrible, terrible trust issues—sometimes even that God really DOES love me and is working out all for my good. I watched Katie walk through such deep, hard, difficult trials—mostly physical—and she rarely cried. She rarely complained or had pity parties. There were times I held her when she cried. But the grace she showed just shone of Jesus. SHONE. She taught me by her example that it was okay to open my heart and trust, especially in my Savior.

Next, she showed me the grace God bestows during suffering. You see, as a Christian sometimes the best things we learn are through suffering. Philippians 3:10 says, "That I may know him, and the power of his resurrection, and the fellowship of his sufferings, being made conformable unto his death." The whole book of Philippians has a theme of suffering, but Paul counteracts it with joy. There are ways we are only going to know Jesus through our suffering, with the reassurance that He suffered first and understands! Katie and I suffered some similar things, so we understood each other in those ways. That bond is the same with our Savior! Katie was the first to help me see that. Did she preach to me about it? Nope. She just lived a life of joy. Even waiting for her to go into brain surgery, we were laughing till we cried. After her surgery, as I was recovering from elbow surgery, we still laughed till we cried!!

The last six months of Katie's life she suffered such physical pain, yet as much as she suffered, when she was better, she went on trips. She travelled. She embraced life. She knew her time on earth would be short. She told Wendy, my other best friend, that. I knew that too in some sense—I knew her medical history. I was always a little worried when she would go travelling; her body was fragile. But she embraced life bigger than anyone I have ever known. Not in a sinful, evil way—just with a joy and exuberance. I guess that would be another example of grace I learned of her—living with JOY. (In case no one has picked up on this, I'm not joyful by nature!) Katie had just come back from a cruise before Easter in 2018 and she came down with a sinus infection. We texted each other on Easter, April 1, 2018. I cannot tell you how many times I have reread those last texts. On April 2, she went to work (she was a nurse as well) and a couple hours into her shift, she asked her charge nurse to check her blood pressure because she felt weak. When her charge nurse got back, Katie was seizing.

Katie's heart gave out that night. They worked on her for 45 minutes, but never got her heart restarted. She had had issues with her heart since she was a teenager; she had already had two ablations for rhythm issues by 26. God finally fixed her broken heart, but only her physical one. Her spirit, her joy, her exuberance will never die for me. I am crying as write these words, recounting the pain of her last moments on earth; but knowing God showered grace on her by allowing her suffering to last only a little while is priceless to me. My friend finished well, and she causes me to want to finish well.

There are thousands of times I have thought of her over the years, and so many times I wished she was here to share a moment with me. I can't make apple butter without thinking of her. That girl could eat my fresh apple butter by the cup—literally! We wore out a gospel CD driving to the beach—she had a beautiful voice; she sang soprano and I sing alto. Wendy would find a place to sing in between or with us. I am so tremendously blessed that God bestowed such grace on me to give me Katie. I look forward to the day that I get to see her once more, forever healed from the physical body that took her too soon. Hug your friends and family. Take the trip. Take the picture. Make memories and love hard. Love without reservation, without hesitation, and fully. Laugh until your sides and face hurt. But mostly, love Jesus and show His love and grace to everyone around you like my Katie did.

Point of reflection: I can't imagine anyone reading this book hasn't dealt with losing someone close to them—death is something that touches everyone. My point of reflection is this: how did that person's death affect you? Did it cause you to cling to Jesus or make you bitter? Have you (eventually) had healing from the pain of loss? Can you look back and see moments of grace even in those days and times when it feels like your world has been shattered?

A couple of verses to comfort you with loved ones in heaven: I Thessalonions 4:13—"But I would not have you to be ignorant, brethren, concerning them which are asleep, that ye sorrow not, even as others that have no hope." Those loved ones who knew Jesus are not hurting anymore or sick—they are HEALED. We have the hope that Jesus has them with Him! Vs. 14 states "For if we believe that Jesus died and rose again, even so them also which sleep in Jesus will God bring with him." Revelation 21:4 states "And God shall wipe away all tears from their eyes; and there shall be no more death, neither sorrow, nor crying, neither shall there be any more pain: for the former things are passed away." The parting we experience is painful but temporary. Last, remember we have a Comforter who the Father gave us that abides with us (John 14:16, paraphrasing mine). We may feel alone or lonely in our loss—but we have the Spirit dwelling in us who gives us all comfort.

CHAPTER FOURTEEN

Life as a Nurse

I JUST DON'T know how to condense and encapsulate how much grace God has showered on me through 20 years of nursing. *20 years* as a critical care, CVICU nurse. My first thought is I just don't know HOW I've done it! My second is most days I do not want to leave. When God put it on my heart to be a CVICU nurse, He gave me a calling. As a friend reminded me not long ago, God gave me a place to minister to people—the opportunities at my job are many to show the love of God to people at a very vulnerable time.

I wish I could say that I do an amazing job at that—I don't. I fail in that pretty much every day. I frequently tell my coworkers that I pray for grace on the way in and forgiveness on the way home. HA! It is so true though!! I've threatened many a morning coming home to just go lay at the altar at church for a couple of hours just getting things taken care of! Some days I feel like I spend half the shift either asking forgiveness or praying for it!

I'm not going to recount specific examples—it would probably come close to a HIPPA violation and quite frankly I need to keep paying my mortgage. But here's what I'll do—I'm going to take a deep breath and try to summarize how God has showered me with grace in the past 20 years.

God graced me with a job, but not just a job. A vocation. A calling. A place to minister. He equipped me for the place He called me to. Let me repeat that again, because it's true no matter where you work—He equipped me for the place He called me to. That is the same if He calls you to sing, preach, wash dishes at a restaurant, be a lawyer, a doctor, or a corporate executive—He will give you what you need to do what He wants you to do!! That doesn't mean you don't have to work. I study, read journal articles, do research when I need to; nursing is not a once and done thing. Just like anywhere else, you'll have to learn new skills and embrace change and new ideas to keep being effective in your job. I think of the verse "Whether therefore ye eat, or drink, or whatsoever ye do, do all to the glory of God." (I Corinthians 10:31). I fail plenty of times. But God made me to give 100% when I do something, and what I do requires that (and sometimes it feels like much more!!).

More times than I can count, God gave me grace in the moment. That hard IV stick or lab draw. A foley placement. A different tube placed…somewhere else. Just the right words to say to a patient or a coworker. When it talks in the Bible about God bringing all things to your remembrance, He surely and absolutely will do so! I can't recall the number of times I've either recalled a verse from long ago that was just what someone else needed to hear, or if it was the still small voice of God calming me so I could keep doing what needed to be done. He gives the strength to get through just one more shift when I don't feel like I could physically do it while I was waiting to get something else fixed.

Let me just add onto that idea for a minute. I know—you're bored of hearing about my poor broken body, but working 20 years and enduring what I've had to during that time while still working? Folks, that is new grace I've not needed before. That's grace on grace. That is God richly supplying my every need, Him being the glory and lifter up of my head (Psalm 3), my weakness in His strength. I could not, even for half of a hot second, have been able to keep going without Him. When your pain as the caregiver is making you break out in a cold sweat and make you lightheaded when you move that patient, or when a patient grabs your arm to steady themselves not realizing your shoulder is torn and you can still keep going—that, my dear friend, is the grace of almighty God and nothing else.

God graces me every day giving me wisdom in hard situations. Answering questions. Trying my best to not only take care of my patients but also help others when they have needed it. Guiding nurses through situations where patients are trying to die, and we are trying to stop them. Let me tell you, folks—if you know a nurse, pray for them to have the wisdom of Solomon and the love of Jesus, the patience of Job, and the longsuffering of someone like Paul. Our job is hard; we need as many people praying for us as possible. God also showers me with grace in being able to compartmentalize. Really, Mel? Is that grace? Almost every nurse who has been on the job for any length of time, especially in the season and setting of Covid, has had to clean up a patient who has died, place them in a body bag, and take them down to the morgue—then turn around and paste a smile on their face and go take care of the next patient. I've had swollen, red rimmed eyes walking into the next patient's room more than once—yet we have to "wall it off" and wait until we have to time to process our own grief and do our best to meet someone else's needs.

God graces me to show mercy when I don't always want to be merciful. He reminds me (mostly before I say something stupid, but sometimes I open my mouth before I listen to Jesus!) how much mercy and grace He has lavished on me—I need to turn around and show that to others! This is where I struggle so badly, to be completely forthright. God forgive me, there are times I struggle to understand people's choices, but I have to remember I have made plenty of terrible ones myself! One of my harder ongoing struggles is with my own pain—there have been moments I've wanted to tell a patient I deal with chronic and sometimes bad flare ups of pain and yet here I am, trying to help you. Harsh? Yup. Honest? To a fault. I tend to swing a pendulum with my empathy—either I am not feeling too bad and so I can be very understanding of others, or I am wracked and my sympathy-o-meter is broken that day. That's when God reminds me, yet again, to "rejoice with them that rejoice and weep with those who weep". (Paraphrased from Romans 12:15) I might not understand why someone is reacting the way they are, but I do know from personal experience if I react with kindness, it has a much more positive affect.

Even in the midst of hard and trying times, God has granted me grace as a nurse. Every nurse who's worked more than, say, five minutes at the bedside (I'm joking—it's not that bad!!) has had some kind of rough moment. I've been yelled at, cursed at, swung at, kicked, spit on, puked on, you name it...most times absolutely accidental (at least with the body fluids, thankfully!)...well, except maybe the cursing... anyhoo...those are the times you need that clear head the most. Being straight cussed out by anyone is hard to deal with, but filtering through at light speed is the question: is this stemming from pain, loss, frustration, or their personality? No matter what, God giving patience and the right word at the right time is grace!! On the flip side, overreacting and yelling back (yup, I've done it!) and then going back and making things right is its own form of grace...grace that the Holy Ghost prodded me and prompted me to ask forgiveness of either a coworker or a patient and seek forgiveness from God. Grace is God giving you a past where you learned to be a peacemaker and a peacekeeper and giving you the ability to smooth out situations. Grace is God giving you wisdom and discernment in split second moments. Grace is God giving you strength after your patient codes and you want to slide down the wall and cry, but you have to get up and try your best to comfort the family. Grace is wrapping your arms around someone weeping from loss and God giving you just those right words...again and again.

God has granted me, time and time again, the ability to be "swift to hear, and slow to speak" (James 1:19). Any failure there, any offense I have caused, is mine alone and not of God. Again, may He forgive me. I know that on occasion speaking of Jesus can cause offense to unbelievers—I still believe in gently and quietly planting the seed of the gospel, even if it's just being a little kinder to that difficult patient and having them ask me why I'm so nice. (I promise it's not me—dear sweet heaven do I have a temper!!) I've also had moments where I felt like I had to defend God to someone who truly did not seem to believe in God; in those moments I've felt the Holy Spirit impress upon me to just be quiet. Those are hard moments; He has done so much for me!! All I can do then is pray that God will soften that person's heart. God has also given me grace in the words to say and actions of love. He has opened doors for me to pray with and for coworkers and patients. If you ask God to open a door and allow you to speak for Him to someone, in His time He will do that! I have tried to obey Him when I felt the Lord nudging me to talk to someone about Him. On the flip side, I know beyond a shadow of a doubt that either a patient or coworker was the one comforting me through Him! I've had more than one patient look at me and say they were praying for me; that means more to me than anything! I do wonder sometimes what the look on my face was that prompted them to start praying. Hope it wasn't fear. Just kidding!! I've been blessed with some amazing coworkers over the past 20 years, many of them I consider amazing friends as well. God sure has been gracious more than I could ask to have such fantastic people to work with. I would like to think I have been a blessing to them, but so much more I know I have been blessed by them; and I know God showered me with grace putting them in my path!!

So many times, God has given me the grace to comfort someone and be comforted. I am so thankful that when Jesus left this earth, He left us a Comforter in His Holy Spirit! Giving comfort to another when you are either hurting yourself or wanting comfort is something of

God—only God can give that ability, I am convinced of it!! But I am *real*. If a family member is crying, I am too. I used to think that I couldn't cry if my patient died. Now? No, that isn't my loved one—but their hurt touches me. Even that, friends, is of God—to take someone who didn't cry for a whole year, who had so much hurt, pain, and bitterness—that is God and His grace and healing, and I am *thankful* and blessed beyond measure for how He has worked in my heart.

Point of reflection: What is your calling? Are you a stay-at-home mom or dad? Are you a construction worker, a healthcare worker, a businessman, in the military? I'm just randomly naming a few. Whatever your job/ calling is…it is your MINISTRY where God has placed you; even if it's a temporary job. I am beyond thankful for my friend who reminded me of this when I was so torn about my job because of how hard it had gotten on me. Truthfully, I had lost sight of that just trying to live through the next shift. I needed that wake-up call to sustain me and sharpen my focus. It's not just saving a life for me, giving pain meds, weaning down meds—it's far bigger than that.

Whatever God has called you to do, do it heartily, as to the Lord, and not unto men (Colossians 3:23). I Corinthians 10:31 states "Whether therefore ye eat, or drink, or whatsoever ye do, do all to the glory of God." This is something I tell my kids—do your best for Him. Will we be perfect? Nope. I can tell if the work I'm doing is just going through the motions or if I am bathing my work life in prayer—it's just different. I pray you will do the same! It doesn't mean it will always be easy—man, can life be hard sometimes! But if we remember from Psalm 37:5a to "Commit thy way unto the Lord; trust also in him" that work and burden are so much easier.

CHAPTER FIFTEEN

What Have I learned about myself?

I HONESTLY THOUGHT, as of January this year, that this book was finished. Complete. I was content with the ending. Well, sort of. Really—knowing myself—would I be? (Clearly the answer is a resounding NO because I'm sneaking in another chapter!)

It's July 11, 2022. It's 3:28 am. (I'm a chronic third shifter so this is not a terribly unusual time for me to be awake, but still…)

Rest would not come. It's been a day. My pastor has been preaching a series about evil and why God allows evil, and it has been a little gut wrenching for me. There are things I haven't revealed in the book that I can't go into detail with, but I have experienced plenty of evil at the hands of those who I should have trusted explicitly. Let's just say the past three weeks at church have worn me out, wrung me dry, and alternately encouraged me and weakened me. When that happens, I'm like anyone else…I'm filled with doubts, I'm prone to the attacks of Satan…whew.

So what has writing this book taught me about myself and my journey of grace?

Such a big first and foremost, I'm not at all worthy of God's grace. Not even a little bit. No more and no less than anyone else. I'm immensely, tremendously thankful. And now I'm crying…again. Seriously, I'm kinda tired of crying. Moving on. Second, I'm a scaredy cat. Yup. I'm still terrified of finishing and publishing this book. I have faced attacks of the evil one writing this book—all completely and thoroughly countered by the almighty grace of God. For every weird thing that I KNEW was Satan moving against me, there would be a move of God to counter it. I'm still crying as I type this. But those attacks of Satan—until I saw them for what they were, I was SCARED.

That being said, I looked up the definition of courage and found some from different dictionaries I drew comfort from. The first is from Merriam-Webster (8), and it states that courage is "mental or moral strength to venture, persevere, and withstand danger, FEAR (emphasis mine), or difficulty." The next was from Oxford Languages (9): courage is "the ability to do something dangerous, or to face pain or opposition, without showing fear." Okaaaaayyy…I guess maybe I've gained some courage, because boy howdy have I been afraid writing this sometimes. The definition "strength in the face of pain or grief" really was the one that encouraged me. I know it's not from the Bible, but maybe, just maybe, that definition will ring true with someone. It's not that you're not afraid—but you DO SOMETHING ANYWAY.

I also found two quotes about courage I really liked. From Franklin D. Roosevelt, "Courage is not the absence of fear, but rather the assessment that something else is more important than fear." (10) From Carly Fiorina, the American businesswoman that ran for president in 2016, "courage is not the absence of fear, courage is acting in spite of fear." (11) Yes. So much yes in these.

I don't find myself particularly brave. Resilient? Stubborn? Yes. Brave? Not so much. But courage? I guess I have that. Or I've found it. People that know me will tell me that I'm amazing…oh my word, I'm not. I'm just…me. And me, most days, doesn't seem like anything special. Remember in the foreword of my book I brought up the example of Moses? Still there. Still not feeling called to lead a nation out of the desert…but you know what? Did Moses feel that calling either? I don't remember reading that in the Bible. What is made clear through Moses's story is God will equip you to what He is calling you to do!! When Moses brought up his difficulty speaking, God already had Aaron, Moses' brother, appointed to help him. Moses already had the staff that would be used throughout Exodus over and over again. My point? If God calls you to do something, He will equip you for that calling. What is God calling me to do next? I'm not certain, but writing this book sure has given me the courage to act in fear and take the next step of obedience.

I'm laying out my fears and failures here…my weaknesses…my heart. This book nearly destroyed me in the writing, but then I've gained healing that I didn't anticipate. (Bless it, I just started crying again. Have I mentioned I'm tired of crying? Moving on…) I have faced down my past; all kinds of trauma (and when I say that, there are all kinds of abuse I have survived…I debated putting that in here, but I now have the guts to name what I survived was abuse. If you try to put a different label on there so it doesn't seem so bad, it's still abuse.), uncovering emotional wounds long buried that I sure didn't want to dredge back through, and forgotten moments that I needed clarity on. I've slogged my way, by God's grace, through knee jerk reactions that stemmed from the past; forced myself to mentally rewrite those reactions and actually heal from those old wounds rather than just let them scar over unhealed. I've made myself face the facts that many of my mistakes stemmed from my knee jerk reactions. I've learned from them…I hope. Doesn't mean I don't live with the consequences from some of them, but moving forward I don't intend to make the same mistakes again.

But what I found the most? (Besides the fact that I'm a survivor, albeit a train wreck of one sometimes…) God's grace and His love can conquer ALL. And I mean that…ALL. There is not one thing that you or I can endure that God will not bring you through. Not. One. Will it be pretty? Will you question why? Will you scream and cry and rant and rave? Yeah…you sure will if you're human. Will you want to curl up in a ball sometimes and feel like you can't keep going? Again, yup. Oh my friends reading this…lean into Jesus. Learn the truths of God and repeat them over and over until you BELIEVE them…God is GOOD. It is His nature, His immutable, unchanging nature. God is LOVE. He cannot NOT be love. But don't forget that God is also HOLY. And we are called, as His children, as Christians, to be set apart and to "Be ye holy, as I am holy" (I Peter 1:16).

I've faced some giants in this writing. I've actually sung a solo… and I'm working on another one. This isn't something I would do except for the grace and strength of God (and a big old act of obedience). My job has shifted somewhat. I'm still a nurse, but I have sort of dual role. Again…God's grace for gifting me these. I still don't enjoy public speaking but it's part of my new job role, and I have to do it—so I'm doing it. I'm sort of amazed how God has reshaped and changed me. I'm bolder in confronting people. I don't just let people hurt me and not speak up. Before, I would just take it on the chin—and I'll still take a lot, don't get me wrong. I still believe some things aren't worth the fight, and I would encourage you to pray before you confront. Let God calm you and give you the words to say before you talk to someone.

One big giant—and I'll struggle with this till the day I die; I have no doubt. Self-worth. One of my favorite passages in the Bible is Psalm 139. The whole chapter. It's all good (the whole Bible is good! You can't go wrong reading it!). I've always taken comfort in knowing God knows my very thoughts—He knows them, and He still loves me. I'm a putz, a jerk, a moron sometimes…when I'm tired or scared, I tend to complain. I've had to confess that sin so many times and yet still, I struggle with it. But He still forgives. I have vacillated many times on publishing this book. I haven't wanted to reveal my deepest hurts, because frankly some days I look back and I don't have a clue how I survived—except for grace. Truly, who wants to lay out all their pain and let others see it? I didn't want to share my testimony, didn't want to lay all of this out there…I honestly didn't see how it could help anyone when I've battled so much bitterness from it over the years. I've struggled mightily to find joy so many times. I've been reshaped, reconfigured, and refined—and that refining hurts like blue blazes sometimes.

Here is some truth though, friends. You can either believe Psalm 139—that you, too, are fearfully and wonderfully made, AS YOU ARE—or you don't. But it's in the Bible. YOU ARE FEARFULLY AND WONDERFULLY MADE. That weakness you struggle with? God intended it. My joints that plague me and give me daily pain? God knew, and He allowed it—it's been so hard to see the good in that, but I can look back (bless it, I'm crying again. Seriously, I need some tissues and maybe some time at the altar again…) and see what He has brought me through and praise Him. I just finished charging the stimulator in my back that allows me to keep working, keep moving…and I'm thankful, SO thankful, that He allowed me to get that, because I might have had to go on disability without it. When I first felt the nudging to write this book, I physically couldn't—my carpal tunnel wouldn't allow me to hold a pen that long, and I had to have surgery on my right shoulder and then my carpal tunnel released before I could start it. But during that time, God protected me from the worst of taking care of Covid patients because I was either out with surgery or was medically removed from taking care of anyone on isolation (I couldn't tie the gowns without risking ruining the repair to my shoulder). So even in that time, God was protecting me over and over again. When I felt that urge from God again to write, I started the book, home because my daughter had gotten covid. Praise His name, she is fine.

I wrote while I was recovering from the stimulator placement. The wound infection that came with it. Four days later repeat knee surgery. Physical therapy. I wrote. It was therapy. I struggled HARD with fearfully and wonderfully made. But during that time, I was incredibly blessed to spend an amazing amount of time with my best friend, since she was recovering from surgery as well. I also was able to spend some time with some dear ladies from church, some old friends and some new. I was able to go to Tennessee and enjoy NQC again and develop brand new friendships. Ain't God good?

I'll leave this chapter with this, since I'm focused so much on courage and healing. Joshua 1:6a states, "Be strong and of a good courage". Verse 7a states "Only be thou strong and very courageous". Verse 9, so often quoted, states "Have not I commanded thee? Be strong and of a good courage; be not afraid, neither be though dismayed; for the LORD thy God is with thee withersoever thou goest." This was God talking to Joshua, who took over as the leader of Israel after Moses died. He was the one who would lead them into the Promised Land. He literally fought battles—real battles with swords and bloodshed. My battles aren't fought with real swords; Ephesians 6:12 states, "For we wrestle not against flesh and blood, but against principalities, against powers, against the rulers or the darkness of this world, against spiritual wickedness in high places." Our battles might be physical at times, but they are spiritual in nature—my mind is my worst battle. Satan knows this. He knows how to wound me, hurt me, cripple me. God forgive me, sometimes it happens, and I don't recognize it in time. But God has given us, multiple times, the command to be COURAGEOUS. Move with fear, friends, but keep moving!!

Psalm 139:14: "I will praise thee: for I am fearfully and wonderfully made: marvellous are thy works, and that my soul knoweth right well." I've encouraged my Awana kids to memorize Psalm 139:1-10. I'm determined to memorize this entire chapter; I've quoted it so much to myself but now I have to determine to BELIEVE it. I often joke about being a train wreck, a hot mess express, a disaster—but I'm not. I've struggled with my weight, my joints, my looks, my talents; I've struggled with panic attacks at being noticed because in years past being noticed got me in some kind of trouble. I'm done with that thinking—I have to be. That doesn't mean I'm going to dress immodestly; but I'm not going to hide. (I can't—I'm 5'10"—it's hard to hide when God made you to stand out.) Some days that will mean my "Sunday church big hair" in a dress with some eye makeup; honestly most days it'll still be yoga pants/shorts/jeans with T shirt/sweatshirt/long sleeved shirt with hair in requisite ponytail/mom bun. I'm not one so much to mess with my hair a lot (I don't know how, honestly—using a diffuser is about my limit) but I'm thankful God blessed me with wavy/curly hair. I'm thankful He gave me good skin since He also (with His sense of humor I guess) made me with sensitive skin and allergic to/sensitive to most makeup. I'm thankful for the blue eyes He blessed me with. I won't apologize anymore for the talents God has blessed me with; rather, I'm going to strive to use them for His glory with everything I've got.

My last point of reflection for this book: what is holding you back from doing what He has called you to do? What healing do you need to do? Are you, too, struggling with believing He made you unique, special, and an amazing creation just as you are? That He made you for a purpose and a plan, and if you obey Him, you can join Him in that plan? Pray, my friends—then listen. Listen to that still small voice; don't listen to the self-defeating voice of the devil whispering to you that you are worthless/useless/used up. If you are still on this earth, God isn't done with you yet.

CHAPTER SIXTEEN

Looking Forward

IT'S JANUARY 23, 2022, at 1:10AM.

I have church in a few hours...I can't wait. I want to worship!

I want to praise Him!! I want to thank Him!

When I started this book in August, I was filled with trepidation. I have learned so much along the way. Read a lot of Scripture. Reflected much. Prayed for hours for the words to say. Wrote and rewrote. Corrected. Changed phrasing. Scratched whole sections out.

Honestly, I still don't have a clue if I'm going to publish this. It's pretty raw, and frankly, I'm not the best with criticism. If I do publish it, please be kind—don't destroy me!! (And if you're reading this now in print, you may correctly assume that I've decided to publish it. You're welcome!)

The format and the style of this book are not always 100% "proper" English. I am aware of that; it was intentional. I wanted it to be casual and informal—kind of like your bestie coming over for coffee and you're both in your jammies. (If you're like my bestie we match our jammies to be obnoxious—please pray for our husbands!!)

What did I want of this book?

I wanted this book to showcase, highlight, and explode with how God's grace has every single day, every single moment enabled me to live and KEEP GOING. I pray it has done that. I've prayed for hours as I've written. I will pray for more hours that the "…words of my mouth, and the meditation of my heart, be acceptable in thy sight, O Lord, my strength, and my redeemer" (Psalms 19:14).

I have been reminded over and over through this book how many times God has shown immeasurable, remarkable, miraculous grace throughout my life—sometimes when I have prayed for it, and others when God in yet another show of grace just blessed me with it without asking!!

And you know what, friends?

I'm going to make it. As Mrs. Brenda, my pastor's wife, sings, He already said that I would. And you will too if you know Him as your Savior—the same grace He has given me and promised me are *yours* as well!! Please, I beg you, if you haven't before—call on Jesus today!!

I know I have mentioned this before, but I love crocheting. (Honestly, as soon as I'm done typing this, I'm going to work on yet another project—sigh…) An amazing object lesson came to me one night as I was crocheting that I want to share. Normally, I work from the middle of a skein of yarn out; sometimes you have a clump of yarn you have to unravel from the very center and after that it's pretty smooth sailing. This particular skein seemed like it wanted to teach me lessons—ha!! Four times while I was trying to pull out some more yarn to work with, I had to stop and carefully, tediously pull apart knots and clumps of yarn. Those will take usually at least 30 minutes to unravel. I would sigh and work through that mess, crochet it through, and lo and behold—it would happen again!! It struck me that that is how life is. So many times, we think we are smooth sailing and we hit a snag, a curveball—and we get stuck trying so hard to "unravel" the mess. We feel like we are losing time, spinning our wheels, just churning mud trying to get through it.

Finally, though, that little "chunk" was unraveled, and we could keep working. Isn't that life? I feel like so many times I have been in those times and my impression, especially looking back, is God was telling me, child—slow down for heaven's sake. Stop working so hard on your own. Stop tugging on life to go where you want or make life "do" what you want. Quit resisting and give in to Me and let Me unravel what seems to be a mess. God can work out our "messes" better than we could even try!! He can take those knots and clumps and then keep working and turn those spots into beauty that will take your breath away if we let Him.

It doesn't matter what tomorrow brings—He is already there. It doesn't matter what happens—He already knew it would happen, and if He allowed it, He will give you the grace to get through it!! I don't have some magic answer as to why He allows some things except to think of the man born blind in the gospels; Jesus's disciples asked if this man or his parents had sinned, and Jesus responded neither, but that the Father would be glorified. I pray that these difficult times I have gone through (and believe me, what I've been through pale in comparison to what others have gone through) will at some point in time point just one more soul to God that He may be glorified!!

Will I cry at times, get frustrated, sad, discouraged, despair—you get the idea—yup. Did tonight, as a matter of fact. Had to step out on faith and call on my Savior; even though nothing miraculously changed, God gave grace and peace. And what was bothering me got so much easier to bear.

No matter what comes next, there will be grace. Praise God for His gift of grace.

About the Author

MELANIE WAS BORN in a small town in southeastern Pennsylvania where she picked up aggressive driving habits and quality Amish cooking abilities. She graduated from Bob Jones University with a Bachelor of Science degree in Pre-Med in 1994. After a brief return to Pennsylvania, she relocated to South Carolina in 1995. She graduated with her Associate's degree in nursing from Greenville Technical College in 2002. She makes her home with her incredibly patient husband Frank and their three daughters, along with three furry kitties who in reality make the household rules. She is still working as a critical care nurse specializing in cardiovascular intensive care. She also has a secondary job role as an ECMO specialist. This is her first foray into the writing world.

You can contact Melanie via email at melaniethurston@bellsouth.net.

References

1. Reye Syndrome, *www.emedicine.medscape.com*, Reye Syndrome, April 2018, Debra L. Weiner, MD, PhD

2. Grace definition and meaning, *www.merriam-webster.com*

3. Grace (Biblical definition), Strong's Concordance 2603

4. This Grace, lyrics by Joseph Habedank, Benji Cowart, and Michael Farren; *Deeper Oceans* CD, 2019.

5. Grace in the Bible, www.gotquestions.org

6. How Saved I Am, words and music by Jason Cox, Scotty Inman, and Kenna Turner West; *Bigger than Sunday* CD, Triumphant Quartet, 2021.

7. New Grace, Dr. Tom Hayes, www.hymnsinmyheart.wordpress.com.

8. Courage definition and meaning, *www.merriam-webster.com*

9. Courage definition and meaning, www.oxfordlearnersdictionaries.com

10. Quote, *www.goodreads.com*

11. Quote, *www.quotefancy.com*

12. As mentioned before, all Bible verses in my book are quoted from the 1611 KJV translation.